CW00434106

* For How to Use This Book see p.15

Exploring Woodland

Peak District & Central England

101 beautiful woods to visit

Collins is an imprint of HarperCollins*Publishers* Ltd.
77–85 Fulham Palace Road
London
W6 8JB

The Collins website address is: www. collins.co.uk

First published in 2002

10 9 8 7 6 5 4 3 2 1

08 07 06 05 04 03 02

ISBN 0 00 714439 3

Site maps produced by Belvoir Cartographics & Design
Site entries written by Sheila Ashton, research by Tim Hill, Diana Moss

Acknowledgements
This publication has been generously supported by the Ernest Cook Trust,
the Forestry Commission, the National Forest Company, the Royal
Forestry Society and Six Continents plc.
Exploring Woodland was initiated as a series by the Forestry Trust whose
work is being continued by the Woodland Trust with the intention of producing guides for all parts of Britain.

Designed by Liz Bourne
Printed and bound by Printing Express Ltd., Hong Kong

INTRODUCTION

Woodland Trust celebrity supporter, Alistair McGowan, says:
'Can you imagine what our countryside would look like without
trees? Sound like a colourless and dreary place? Woods offer us
peace and tranquillity, inspire our imagination and creativity, and
refresh our souls. A land without trees would be a barren, cold
and impoverished place. When I want to get back in touch with
nature and escape from the hustle and bustle of my daily life, I
love to visit and explore these natural treasures. These places are
rich in wildlife and support a wide variety of animal and plant life.
This excellent series of Woodland Trust guidebooks charts some
of the most spectacular woods across the UK. You will be amazed
and inspired to discover the wide variety of cultural and ecological
history that exists in these special places. Each guide provides you
with the all the information you will ever need.'

PEAK DISTRICT AND CENTRAL ENGLAND

Tread softly through the dappled shade of the forest. Keep your wits about you. Stop. Crouch down. Motionless beneath the bracken fronds sense the all enfolding woodland life. Small birds chatter and squabble in the understorey and a jay shouts the odds through the canopy. A drowsy pollen-laden bumble bee blunders hopefully between the swaying foxgloves and close by some unseen rodent rustles through the detritus of the forest floor seeking tasty morsels. There's nothing to be frightened of here, nothing to hide from, but the sunlight tirelessly plays tricks with the shadows. At a glance a bent gnarled old forester, but an instant later the decrepit carcass of a venerable old oak glimpsed beyond the slender silver stems of young birches.

Wood mouse rustles through the forest floor

Robin Hood and his merry band may be merely distant memories of legend and hearsay, locked well away in the 12th or 13th century, but their medieval presence seems to be just out of sight in the next glade, particularly in Birklands; perhaps the finest remaining part of the vast sprawl of Sherwood Forest, which once covered 100,000 acres and stretched for some 40km (25 miles) north of Nottingham. Now part of the Sherwood Forest Country

Major Oak, Sherwood Forest

Park this is still one of the most extensive and atmospheric of ancient oak woods in the Midlands.

Some of the ancient oaks are up to 1,000 years old and, although many are decaying, they still stake a marvellous sculptural presence. They also provide outstanding habitats for all manner of bats, birds and insect life. In fact the area received its Site of Special Scientific Interest (SSSI) designation on the strength of its insects – more than 200 different spiders and almost 1,500 different beetles, some of which are unique to this site. The undoubted star of the forest is the Major Oak, now hollow and partly reliant on a network of props, hawsers and spars to hold it together. Estimated to be about 800–1,000 years old it receives well over 800,000 visitors every year. A few years ago you could clamber all over this senior citizen of the forest, but visitor pressure was beginning to take its toll, so now you must view from a respectful distance.

Sherwood may be one of the highest profile woods in the Midlands, but the area has much else to offer. The general wood-

Wych Elm

land type of oak with birch is one that proliferates throughout the central part of Nottinghamshire and also reaches to the eastern edges of Staffordshire, although it manifests in several different guises. At its finest the mature oaks, which will be prized by foresters for their timber, form the principal canopy with birch, the great coloniser, filling in the gaps caused by felling or natural decline. Coppice woods, cut on a 10–15 year rotation, contain a strong mix of oak, hazel and birch, with a scattering of rowan, field maple and holly. Some of these woods will have a few selected oaks which will be left as standards. On the poorest soils the oak and birch partnership is accompanied by Scots pine in an altogether more open woodland structure. Ash and field maple is the other most common type of woodland of the heavier clay soils of Nottinghamshire, whilst wych elm can be found on the more calcareous soils.

The soil types across this East Midland region vary a great deal which is reflected by the dominant tree and plant species across the range. It is difficult to be categorical about the vegetation in any rigidly defined areas of the Midlands as there are a variety of bedrock incursions throughout the area. However there are a few distinctive woodland types linked to the geology of the region.

The Peak District of Derbyshire, lies on carboniferous limestone; noted for its ash woods with associated wych elm and sycamore. Hazel is the most abundant shrub layer species, whilst hawthorn, rowan, field maple, whitebeam, dogwood, blackthorn, bird cherry and yew all feature strongly. By contrast there are tracts of gritstone here as well, Padley Gorge being a prime example of typical woodland, which supports oak and birch with some Scots pine and beech. The oak and birch mix also prevails on to the bunter sandstones found in Nottinghamshire (see below). The Leicestershire woodland are relatively sparse, with perhaps the most interesting sites to be found on the chalky boulder clays in the south east, where woods tend to be composed mainly of an oak, ash and field maple mix, with shrubs such as elder, blackthorn, privet, and hawthorn forming the attendant understorey. On the eastern fringes of Leicestershire and through into Lincolnshire the prevailing Jurassic rocks manifest in calcareous blue clay or chalk, supporting woodlands of oak, ash, wych elm

Millstones at Padley Gorge

and in several sites considerable amounts of small-leaved lime; the latter being one of the principal species of the ancient wildwood.

Identifying rare species or site status indicators is all part of the fun of exploring woodland, and small-leaved lime is one tree that is a strong indicator of ancient woodland. Pollen records reveal that this tree was once one of the pre-eminent species of lowland woods, but a combination of ancient woodland loss to agricultural improvement, climatic changes which have seen a decline in its ability to set viable seed and its susceptibility to intensive grazing has seen its decline. Where lime is found in woods it is most usually seen as coppice stools, and some of these can be of huge proportions indicating extremely great age. Some of the most venerable stools forming rings of stems 3–6m (10–20ft) in diameter may be several thousand years old, making them potentially the oldest trees in Britain – even older than the most ancient churchyard yews!

It's important to realise that the woodland in evidence today is but a fragment of the almost continuous tree cover, which has been described as wildwood, which once stretched far and wide across Britain. From Neolithic times onwards people cleared trees in order to till the land and graze livestock; the cut timber provided fences to contain these animals, construction material for houses and a regular supply of firewood. Not all this led to the

Traditional management,
Nor Wood, Cook Spring
and Owler Carr

Ancient woodland

dramatic demise of woodland, for it didn't take the intellect of a genius to realise that without allowing some of the woodland to regenerate there would be a finite supply of timber and coppice wood; moreover the fact was, and still is, that it's extremely difficult to obliterate broadleaf woodland simply by cutting it back. No sooner has a tree been cut than it begins to send out new shoots, a process harnessed in coppice and pollard management. Only the truly draconian measure of setting about trees with bulldozers will eradicate them completely and, sadly, this was often the fate of ancient woodland which was seen to be in the way of 'progress'. Unfortunately ancient woodland, Britain's rainforest, our richest habitat for wildlife, is still lost to development today.

During the 18th and early-19th centuries many of the great landowners actually made major contributions to woodland regeneration, partly because they realised the potential revenue to be gleaned from commercial forestry, but they also planted coverts to house their game and vast tracts of parkland to impress their neighbours and friends. The relentless tide of industrial progress on through the 19th century brought pressure to bear on woodland since vast quantities of coppice wood were required for charcoal and tan bark, but by the end of that century much had changed with the eclipsing of timber and charcoal as fuel in favour of coal and coke, and this, coupled with the expansion of agriculture, began to change the hitherto relatively stable status of woodland.

Many of the larger broadleaf trees in today's woodland were planted in the mid-19th century with some purpose in mind, but with subsequent social and economic changes they were no longer needed. In many cases this has provided a legacy of handsome timber trees, but sometimes at the expense of coppice wood or understorey diversity.

The most ambitious woodland project to emerge in the Midlands in recent years has been the creation of the new National Forest, which aims to plant and maintain a great swath of woodland from east Staffordshire through south Derbyshire and north west Leicestershire where the landscape was previously dominated by the industrial sprawl of one of the country's largest coalfields. Now, working in close harmony with local landowners

Douglas fir cones

Sulphur tuft fungi

and the enthusiastic support of local communities the seeds have been sown, or rather the saplings have been planted, of a whole new landscape and amenity for the future.

Take a walk in many a woodland which lies on accessible land and you'll almost certainly discover some degree of introduced conifers. Broadly speaking the most popular species have been Corsican pine, Norway spruce, Sitka spruce, Douglas fir, Western red cedar, and of course the native Scots pine, whilst oak, ash and beech have been popular hardwood choices. Even if your walk takes you through pure broadleaf woods it's quite likely that much of the tree cover will have been managed at some time, or will be the retained standards of an earlier generation of foresters. To find anything remotely approaching natural ancient woodland you must seek out those almost inaccessible locations, where man has always found it difficult to harvest timber and his sheep and cattle have made few inroads with their relentless grazing. Here, natural regeneration creates vibrant woodland containing trees of various ages. Some of the best such examples are the steeper ash woods of the Derbyshire valleys, which are probably little changed over thousands of years.

In some woods you'll find rivers or streams with the mosses, lichens and liverworts which such damp areas support, along with quaint little birds like dippers and wagtails bobbing from rock to rock. Water may exist in the form of ponds, either naturally occurring, or as the relict of some long forgotten industry, and here it may be possible to find breeding colonies of frogs or newts whilst exotic looking dragonflies patrol the surface. For the wettest of woodland sites look for the name Car or Carr (a name derived from the Anglo Saxon for such woods). Alder is usually the dominant species here, although there are also willow carrs. Tattershall Carrs in Lincolnshire, a SSSI, is a splendid example although, in this case, a trifle drier than it might once have been due to extensive drainage systems to aid the surrounding agriculture.

Many woods with the best access contain wide rides cut through the tree cover which encourage butterflies and a greater variety of flowers. Carpets of wood anemones or bluebells are a glorious sight to behold in the spring, but the committed flower

Bluebells at Burroughs Wood

Catkin laden hazel

fanatic can find all manner of rarities in specific woods. You will rejoice the first time you come upon a scarce orchid or find a distinctive plant such as herb-paris or lily-of-the-valley; look to chalky soils for these specialities. With patience you can seek a wonderful array of birdlife; after all woods are the most diverse habitats for nesting birds. Find holes in trees for example, then wait and see what comes or goes. You might catch one of our three splendid woodpeckers or an owl. In the evenings watch for the emergence of several species of bats, or lie low to wait for badgers, foxes and deer to emerge.

Woodland may harbour some remarkable treasures of nature, but also conceals some surprising and fascinating historical evidence. The woods at Beacon Hill Country Park, in Leicestershire, surround what was once a Bronze Age settlement. Evidence of woodland protection in the shape of old boundary ditches and woodbanks often harks back to medieval times. No good having a productive coppice wood if your livestock invade it and graze off all the new growth! Holes in the ground usually relate to some kind of quarrying, often of considerable antiquity or, occasionally, old saw pits where foresters once cut their felled timber with mammoth two-man saws. Padley Woods, for example, contain evidence of quarrying for millstone grit – some of the old millstones still lying forgotten on the old quarry floor. Shallower depressions or, in some hillside woods, small platforms may indicate the past presence of charcoal hearths. Scrape a little surface loam away and discover the black evidence beneath.

So, when's the best time to head off into the woods? Well, any time; no matter what season there's always something different to see. Winter woodland on a chilly electric blue day when hoar frost has picked out every last leaf and twig, or snow lies deep and crisp and even, casting a spell of muffled serenity. Early spring and golden catkin laden hazels glow like beacons as a stiff breeze propels you along the woodland path. Spring also turns the woodland floor into a mass of colour as flowers burst into bloom. Summer's myriad greens paint the canopy canvas and the heady scent of lime blossom fills the evening air inducing slumbers; or rustle and crunch into the pungent smell of autumn with its fireglow show.

Where you choose to go and what you want to see is down to you, and this book helps you make an informed decision. Most of the sites are managed to a greater or lesser degree, which means that rather than trying to dive into some tangled thicket you're assured of good access.

Archie Miles

GLOSSARY

Coppice: A tree or shrub which has been cut close to ground level and then grows a crop of branches which can be harvested in future years. Also known as underwood.

Pollard: A tree cut 2–4m (6½–13ft) above ground level producing a crop of branches, out of reach of browsing animals, which can be harvested in subsequent years.

Ancient Woodland: Woodland that dates from before 1600AD. As tree planting was not widely undertaken before that time, it is probable that ancient woodland dates back many thousands of years.

HOW TO USE THIS BOOK

Covering a region that encompasses the Peak District and central England, this book is divided into four areas represented by key maps on pp.16–17, 34–35, 50–51 and 68. In the pages following the key maps, the sites nearest one another are described together (wherever possible) to make planning a day out as rewarding as possible.

For each site entry the name of the nearest town is given, followed by road directions and the grid reference of the site entrance. The area of the site (in hectares (HA) followed by acres) is given next together with the official status of the site where appropriate (see below). The owner, body or organisation responsible for maintaining the site is given next. The following symbols are used to denote information about the site and its facilities.

Type of Wood
🔲 Mainly broadleaved woodland
🔺 Mainly coniferous woodland
🔲 Mixed woodland

Car Park
Ⓟ Parking on site
🅿 Parking nearby
🚫 Parking difficult to find

Status
AONB Area of Outstanding Natural Beauty
SSSI Site of Special Scientific Interest

Site Facilities
🪧 Sign at entry
ℹ Information board
♿ Less abled access
🐕 Dogs allowed
⬚ Waymarked trail
🚻 Toilet
⛱ Picnic area
£ Entrance charge
🍴 Refreshments on site

Todmorden

A681

A671

Littleborough

Rochdale

A646

W E S T   Y O R K S H

Halifax   26   27   28

A58   25 Dewsbury   40

24

23 *M62*

22 *A640*   **Huddersfield**

A672

21

20

19

Oldham

A635

A62

Holmfirth

A6024   *A616*

A679

GREATER

MANCHESTER

M60

11

12

Stockport

Glossop

A624

Longdendale Estate p.18

Shire Hill p.18

Tom Wood p.19

Snake Woodlands p.20

A57

Upper Derwent Woodlands p.20

Bluebell Wood p.21

A625

Peak District

A5004

Buxton

Macclesfield

A54

Congleton

Biddulph

A53

Leek

A52

Warslow

S O U T

Bitholmes Wood p.22

Wyming Brock p.2

Ecclesha Woods p.2

Padley Gorge p

Burrs Wood p.25

Baslow

Stand Wood p.25

D E R B Y S

National Park

Matlock

A5012

A515

Wirksworth

Longdendale Estate

STALYBRIDGE

From A57 in Glossop, take B6105 and follow road alongside reservoirs to car park and National Park Information Centre at Torside. (SK008975)

350HA (865 ACRES) AONB

UNITED UTILITIES

There is a fairytale quality to Wildboar Clough which makes it a wonderful place to take children who love the small scale of the site, a remnant of the oak and birch woodland that once covered much of the Peak District.

Something of a rarity, the woodland is particularly interesting as well as attractive, with a path winding uphill between stunted oaks and boulders while a small stream cascades down the rock-strewn ravine. It is a great place to explore and enjoy the views across the reservoirs and moorlands beyond. Within the small and quickly explored woodland there are more open areas, which add to the interest.

Entry is via the well-surfaced Longendale Trail, part of the Trans-Pennine Trail, which is suitable for wheelchair use although the woodland itself is not. The woodland path climbs up the site of the clough to an open moor where vegetation includes bracken, heather and bilberry. The route is not difficult but boots are recommended.

Shire Hill

GLOSSOP

From Glossop take A57 Snake Pass. Turn left before leaving Glossop into Woodcock Grove (signposted Pyegrove Estate and Shire Hill). Follow road through the Estate to car park. There is a footpath leading to wood. (SK048944)

30HA (73 ACRES) AONB

PEAK DISTRICT NATIONAL PARK AUTHORITY

Shire Hill is something of a tranquil gem in the heart of an urban area. A drive through a housing estate to a car park and children's play area is followed by a walk across a football field and then up a steep, uneven narrow path on the edge of a housing estate.

But once you enter the wood, the environment quickly changes, for this ancient woodland of birch and oak has a lovely atmosphere, particularly when bathed in afternoon sun. Trees cover the side of the hill and it feels safe and quiet, ideal for local walks or a short visit after crossing the Pennines. The Trans Pennine cycle route runs to the north of the wood along the Roman road and links to the Pennine Way.

Tracks and small paths meander through the wood, drawing you to the top of the hill where the landscape changes to heathland, with fine views.

Tom Wood

GLOSSOP
Take A626 between Glossop and Hollingworth towards Charlesworth. Wood is off Woodseats Lane.
(SJ998930)
11HA (28 ACRES)
THE WOODLAND TRUST

The steep terrain and largely undeveloped character of Tom Wood make it a rewarding place to explore – with care – and a great destination for those seeking a morning or afternoon trip to the country-side. The reward is a beautiful landscape with ash, oak, birch and sycamore, often balanced with a good display of varied wild flowers.

The woodland has a truly rural feel, lining the steep sides of a large bowl-shaped valley in the heart of flat farmland. It forms a clear landmark from the surrounding villages, hills and roads, making it a little surprising given that Manchester is very close by.

The steep slopes can become very muddy so sturdy footwear should be worn, whatever the time of year.

South Yorkshire Community Forest

The South Yorkshire Forest is a mix of open spaces, woodland, wetland, farmland, meadow and urban areas, covering 396km^2 (153 sq. miles). The Forest includes the south of Barnsley, takes in most of Rotherham and the north, south and east of Sheffield. It aims to make access to the countryside easier for all, develop green links to connect the urban areas with the countryside and protect and create areas for wildlife.

Snake Woodlands

GLOSSOP

Take A57 from Glossop or Sheffield.
Park in Birchin Clough layby.
(SK109915)
152HA (376 ACRES) AONB
FORESTRY COMMISSION

The woodland trails leading
down steep-sided valleys
through spruce and larch plantations can get a little
monotonous, especially when
following forest tracks. But the
best of them follow the river
which provides most of the
interest on this site. There are
some pleasant glades along the
river and one of the river trails
leads through an open valley
with moorland vegetation where
you can enjoy a picnic and the
views.

Walking is generally easy-to-
moderate but the steps from the
road to the start of the trails are
fairly steep and the stone-
surfaced path can get slippery
when wet. The blue trail will
take around one-and-a-half
hours, the white trail an hour.
The trails are also likely to get
muddy in the rain – so go armed
with wellingtons!

Although perhaps not really
worth a special trip on its own
merit, Snake Woodlands is well
worth including in a longer walk
– to Kinder Scout (the highest
peak in the National Park) perhaps – or as an alternative to a
moorland walk in poor weather.

Upper Derwent Woodlands

SHEFFIELD

Visitor centre is off A57 west of Sheffield.
(SK173893)
814HA (2012 ACRES) AONB SSSI
SEVERN TRENT WATER

Anyone wishing to see how
mature conifer plantations can
be managed to create attractive
woodland environments would
be well advised to visit the
Upper Derwent Woodlands.

Commercially managed, the
large swathes of woodland surrounding the reservoirs are
dominated by conifers but
much of this is mature and well
thinned – creating a pleasant
walking environment.

Facilities throughout the
valley are excellent, including
the visitor centre at Fairholmes
where the bird-feeding station
provides a wonderful opportunity to view woodland birds.
Three waymarked trails start
out from Fairholmes but those
who prefer can plan their own
exploration of the site along a
good network of footpaths.

Open moorland and reservoir shores are also there to be discovered. Interestingly the dams were used as practice areas by the famed 'Dambusters' during the Second World War – more information is provided in a museum at the west side of Derwent Dam.

Bluebell Wood

NEW MILLS
From A6015 in village of Hayfield turn into Station Road and left into Hayfield village car park. From A624 follow signs for Sett Valley Trail. (SK035869)
4HA (10 ACRES) AONB
DERBYSHIRE COUNTY COUNCIL

As its name suggests, the Bluebell Wood is most notable for the carpet of bluebells it produces in the spring. It's a small, intimate and accessible wood – the perfect spot to take young children for a spring visit and an interesting diversion for Sett Valley trail walkers.

The wood features mixed broadleaves including oak, ash, beech and sycamore with alder and crack willow in its wetter, western end. You'll encounter the lesser celandine and yellow pimpernel and marsh marigold in the wetter parts.

It's great for spring birdsong, though birds aren't seen in large numbers. Nevertheless, green and great spotted woodpeckers, nuthatch, willow warbler and chiffchaff have all been recorded with kingfishers and dippers spotted on the River Sett nearby.

Though not yet suitable for less abled access (plans are in hand) a narrow winding path provides an interesting route through the wood, past a small stream and pond.

below:
Bluebell Wood

Bitholmes Wood

SHEFFIELD
The woodland straddles the main A6102
Sheffield to Huddersfield road just
north of Oughtibridge and south of
Stocksbridge. (SK293965)
33HA (82 ACRES)
THE WOODLAND TRUST

Wharncliffe Woods

SHEFFIELD OR CHAPELTOWN
From A61 turn west towards
Grenoside. Take Woodhead Road north
through village. Wood is on left hand
side once through village. (SK324951)
456HA (1,127 ACRES)
FORESTRY COMMISSION

Robust scenery, open
moorland, steep terrain and
streams make a delightful
backdrop for Wharncliffe (and
Greno) Woods – an enjoyable
family outing destination.

Part of the South Yorkshire
Forest, the woodland has an
interesting history. Wharn is a
corruption of quern, a
handmill used for grinding
grain. In medieval times
Wharncliffe Chase was part of
a royal hunting park and more
recently coal and gannister
were mined here. In Greno
Wood, stone was mined for
buildings.

You'll find traces of all these
activities in the mix of
woodland and fields. Though
much of the area was planted
with conifers after the Second
World War, signs of ancient
oak and birch woodland are
everywhere. Greno Wood has
a number of Corsican pine
compartments and extensive
heathland with ling, bilberry,
broom and gorse. Birch and
oak are regenerating here.

All-terrain bikers, horse
riders and walkers all get a fair
share of access routes though
most are generally strenuous.

Rivelin Valley

SHEFFIELD
From A61 at Owlerton take A6101.
Follow road over B6079 and towards
Malinbridge. Wood is on right once
passed through Malinbridge.
(SK324888)
100HA (247 ACRES)
SHEFFIELD CITY COUNCIL

The Rivelin Valley forms a
wonderfully green corridor
which stretches towards the
stunning Peak District and
provides some wonderful
walks along the riverside.

Here you can look out for
wildlife such as dipper and
heron or explore the history of

right:
Rivelin Valley

the area. For right up until the 20th century, the River Rivelin was used to power grinding mills. You should see ample evidence of the area's industrial heritage along your walk, in the form of dams, mill ponds and weirs.

The main path along the valley is suitable for the majority of users but it can become muddy, even boggy, in wet weather so extra care must be taken.

Wyming Brook

SHEFFIELD
Car park opposite entrance on A57.
(SK268867)
65HA (161 ACRES) SSSI
SHEFFIELD CITY COUNCIL (MANAGED BY
SHEFFIELD WILDLIFE TRUST)

left:
Burrs Wood

Padley Gorge

Dronfield or Bakewell
Take B6521 towards Calver. From A623
turn onto B6001 at Calver and then
B6521 in Grindleford towards station.
Park at station. (SK257799)
25HA (62 ACRES) AONB SSSI
The National Trust

The ancient woodland that lies against the dramatic backdrop of Padley Gorge is recognised as being one of the best sessile oak woods in the south Pennines. It makes a great family destination, contrasting with the classic limestone gorge and woodland at Dovedale, and also has plenty to keep the keen naturalist interested.

This site also boasts an interesting history. The gritstone used to be quarried for the millstones from which the area gets its name and one can be seen next to the path at the top end of the wood, to the south east of the river.

Walking through the site is generally easy, though some of the paths can be more difficult near the top of the woodland and while some paths are stone-surfaced, they can get muddy and slippery – so walking boots are strongly advised.

For a good picnic spot, take the circular walk from Grindleford Station along the river, cross the footbridge to the open country above the woodland and cross down to the other side of the gorge to take in the contrast between shady woodland and open moorland.

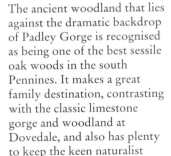

Burrs Wood

UNTHANK
Take B6051 to Milthorpe and turn off to
Unthank. Entrance just through
Unthank on right. (SK305755)
13HA (33 ACRES)
THE WOODLAND TRUST

Scenic and largely unspoilt,
Burrs Wood is a peaceful place
to explore, despite its proximity to Sheffield and
Chesterfield, both of which lie
just 16km (10 miles) away. This
ancient woodland covers the
valley sides of a small stream
on the edge of the stunning
Peak District National Park.

Oak dominates and some of
the more mature specimens are
probably well over 200 years
old. There is also birch, rowan,
a scattering of ash, elder and,
near the roadside, elms.
Enormous coppice stools indicate regular coppicing once
took place here. Conifers were
planted in the late 19th century
but today only larch remains.

Burrs Wood has an
abundance of attractive and
well-loved wild flowers including bluebells, wood-sorrel,
creeping jenny, ramsons and
meadowsweet. Fox and grey
squirrel may be seen.

Stand Wood

BAKEWELL
Follow brown signs to Chatsworth,
which is 13km (8 miles) north of
Matlock off the B6012. (SK259702)
96HA (237 ACRES) AONB
THE CHATSWORTH ESTATE

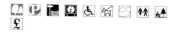

Stand Wood at Chatsworth is a
19th-century romantic landscape
adventure playground that is still
delighting visitors in the 21st
century. The real 'pièce de résis-
tance' is a man-made dell with an
elaborate waterfall.

Used by local people, this is a
well managed woodland with
both timber and aesthetic value.
The site is a mixture of young
pine and beech hilltop
plantations contrasting with the
main areas of mature beech and
oak with sections of yew, elm
and holly.

Surfaced roads and
waymarked tracks wend their
way through the wood, which is
generally fine for all ages and fit-
ness levels but the terrain is quite
steep and not really suitable for
the less abled. Rocky outcrops
provide consistent reminders that
the wood is in the heart of the
gritstone Peak. The waymarked
main paths could be used as part
of an enjoyable longer walk
between Baslow and Beeley.

Linacre Woodlands

CHESTERFIELD
Located off B6050 west of Cutthorpe.
(SK335728)
81HA (200 ACRES)
SEVERN TRENT WATER

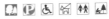

Everyone, from grandparents to tots, can find something to enjoy in Linacre Woodlands, be it the woodland mix, its three reservoirs, multitude of wildlife or the regular events. This is a very popular site but large enough not to look crowded and served by a series of well laid out car parks nestling in pockets of woodland. Large layout plans in each car park highlight a series of walks and circular routes around the reservoirs.

The woods themselves are a mixture of conifers – larch and pine concentrated on the southern fringe – and broadleaves which populate the woods with oak, beech, ash, birch and holly.

A clearing has been used to create a demonstration area where seasonal aspects of woodland management are explained and elsewhere on the path edges a number of information boards describe the history of the reservoir and woodland.

The woodland attracts a wide variety of wildlife habitats and there is usually a warden on hand who will point out aspects of seasonal interest.

The good variety of walks along well-maintained paths follow the valley upstream, changing to boardwalks in spots where the path cuts into the water's edge, and lead to the top end of the site which tends to be the quietest and where you can enjoy excellent views across the valley. This area is a designated conservation site, with cycles excluded and dogs permitted only when on a lead.

above left:
Linacre Woodlands

left:
Eccleshall Woods (p.28)

Eccleshall Woods

SHEFFIELD

Travelling along A621 turn west at
Beauchief traffic lights onto Abbey
Lane. (SK323824)

140HA (346 ACRES)

SHEFFIELD CITY COUNCIL

Eccleshall Woods is the largest
ancient woodland site in the
Sheffield area and has a
wonderful array of wildlife.
Spring visitors can enjoy the
dazzling site of carpets of bluebells on the woodland floor
and the keen eyed might even
spot all three British native
woodpecker species in the
wood – the great spotted, lesser
spotted and green woodpecker.

Walking conditions are generally very good. Exploration
of the site is made possible
thanks to an extensive network
of public footpaths and bridleways. There is also a special
trail for less able people.

There is a lot to discover
including charcoal heaths, a
wood collier's grave, old coppice stools and some magnificent stands of over-mature
beech.

Forest Plantation

WORKSOP

B6045 south of Blyth, turn right going
south immediately at sign 'Hodsock
Farms'; going north pass Hundred Acre
Wood, 1.6km (1 mile) further on left.
(SK616844)

15HA (37 ACRES)

SIR ANDREW BUCHANAN BT.

Eaton Wood

RETFORD

From A638 at Eaton take minor road
from Eaton to Upton. Wood is about
half way between Eaton and Upton.
(SK727772)

25HA (62 ACRES)

NOTTINGHAMSHIRE WILDLIFE TRUST

Historic Eaton Wood is mentioned in the Domesday Book
and is worthy of note for its
flora – particularly its impressive spring display of bluebells
and primroses followed by
orchids – and its fairytale quality.

Ancient in origin, it stands
on a prominent ridge yet is
quietly tucked away and
secluded, despite its proximity
to the A1. The silence is
usually punctuated only by the
sound of the London to
Edinburgh main line express.

Low-key but well-marked
paths lead through a good variety of habitats including
thinned and newly coppiced
areas where you may even see

charcoal being made.

The main tree species are oak, ash, birch and sycamore with planted beech and conifers, which are gradually being removed. There is a dense under-storey of hawthorn, blackthorn and field maple providing wildlife shelter. You might spot a deer or disturb a woodcock.

Nor Wood, Cook Spring and Owler Car

DRONFIELD

Take A61 south from Sheffield for about 8km (5 miles) then turn left onto the B6056 to Eckington for approx 1km (⅔ mile). Turn left down Owler Car Lane. Entrance 30m down lane on left. (SK371805)

31HA (76 ACRES) SSSI

THE WOODLAND TRUST

There's a rural feel to Nor, Cook Spring and Owler Car Woods, despite their proximity to Sheffield, about 3km (2 miles) away. It's not surprising local residents enjoy relaxing here.

The woods form part of a larger complex that includes Coalpit Wood, Newfield Spring Wood and Whinacre Wood and has a long history of human use. Once surface mined, the area was cleared and replanted with non-native species – larch, red oak, maple and sycamore. But there is still a good year-round variety of flora and fauna including ferns, bluebells, dog's mercury and barren strawberry which loves hedge-banks and clearings. Today most trees are native including oak and ash high forest with a wild cherry, holly and hazel understorey.

Part of Cook Spring Wood has Site of Special Scientific Interest (SSSI) designation as one of Derbyshire's most unchanged oak woodland.

Owler Car once had some 25 white coal hearths, hinting that lead smelting may have taken place during the last century. Coppice stools suggest charcoal burning also took place.

left:
Clumber Park

Clumber Park

WORKSOP
Follow A614 (off A1) and take first
turning on right (at Apleyhead Lodge).
(SK645773)
539HA (1332 ACRES) SSSI
THE NATIONAL TRUST

Enter Clumber Park from
Apleyhead Lodge and you
enter another world, with an
incomparable double avenue of
limes stretching ahead – stunning in summer or winter and
exceptional in spring.

A good number of interesting trails take you through the
heath, birch and oak woodland
and conifer plantations that
make up the site, which
features a year-round
programme of events.

Most people are drawn to
the lake. An excellent circular
walk takes in a variety of sights
and habitats. On the southern
shore, work is underway to
clear rhododendron and open
up views to an assortment of
follies, ruins and a slightly for-
bidding Gothic revival chapel.
Surrounding this is a mini-
arboretum.

Cyclists are encouraged to
use the park via a good network
of cycle routes and bikes can
be hired on site. Alternatively,
explore quieter sections from a
network of paths and
bridleways. Also worth a visit
is the newly refurbished
organic kitchen garden.

Kirton Wood

OLLERTON

From A6075 take road to Egmanton.
Wood approx half way between Kirton
and Egmanton. (SK707687)

20HA (49 ACRES) SSSI

NOTTINGHAMSHIRE WILDLIFE TRUST

One of the striking features of
Kirton Wood is the uniform
size of the trees – the result of
the site being cleared half a
century ago. Bought by the
Wildlife Trust in 1985, the ash
and wych elm wood is a designated Site of Special Scientific
Interest (SSSI) and is also rich
in hazel, hawthorn, field maple
and dogwood.

Flowers such as wood
anemone, sweet woodruff,
primrose, ramsons, yellow
archangel and early-purple
orchid confirm the ancient
status of the wood. You can
also find common spotted and
butterfly orchids, and
bluebells.

Visitors can take advantage
of guided walks of the site – by
arrangement – to explore the
variety of rides and look out
for butterflies such as common
blue, brimstone, orange tip and
comma – or birds like the sparrowhawk, blackcap, spotted
flycatcher and great spotted
woodpecker.

Boughton Brake

OLLERTON

Directly adjacent to Boughton pumping
station (see brown tourist signs on
A614). (SK669692)

47HA (116 ACRES)

FORESTRY COMMISSION

below:
*Nor Wood, Cook Spring and Owler
Car (p.29)*

Sherwood Forest Country Park

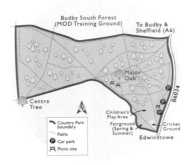

OLLERTON OR EDWINSTOWE
Situated on B6034, north of
Edwinstowe. Signposted from M1 north
and south and the A1 with brown
tourist signs. (SK626678)
181HA (447 ACRES) SSSI
NOTTINGHAMSHIRE COUNTY COUNCIL

Any child who has dreamed of
Robin Hood and his famous
haunts in Sherwood Forest
couldn't fail to be delighted by
the modern day Sherwood
Forest Country Park. It simply
has all the ingredients you need
for a great family day out –
including the famous Major

above:
*Sherwood Forest
Country Park*

Oak, Birkland ancient oak wood and even the men in green themselves!

Good visitor facilities, ample car parking, a fun programme of events in the summer and excellent information all add to the Sherwood Forest experience. But there is so much more to be derived from visiting this area and children are quick to tap into their own imaginations as they explore this ancient woodland.

Well-surfaced paths radiate from the centre, including a round trip for those making the 'pilgrimage' to the Major Oak. As you explore the woodland you become aware of vast numbers of gnarled veteran oak trees (996 at the last count) which are carefully monitored yet allowed to retain a wild and eerie quality.

If you venture away from the marked paths you will enter heathland, developing woodland and a patchwork of scrub and rough grassland, which creates an area rich in invertebrate species. Birds recorded on site include crossbills, long-eared owls, sparrowhawk, redstart, nightjar and all three British native woodpecker species.

A number of footpaths cross the area, including a medium distance walk called the 'Robin Hood Way' while cyclists can take the Sustrans cycle route to access Clumber in the north or Sherwood Pines in the south.

below:
*Sherwood Forest
Country Park*

Peak District

A625

A5004

Buxton

Baslow

Macclesfield

D E R B Y

A54

National Park

Congleton

A5012

Biddulph

Warslow

A53

Leek

Castern Wood p.46

Black Rocks p.4
Wirkswo

A52

A515

Coombes Valley p.46

Dovedale p.47

Carsington Water p.43

A5009

A524

Harston Wood p.48

A5

Newcastle-under-Lyme

Cotton Dell p.49

Ashbourne

Stoke-on-Trent

Cheadle

Dimmings Dale p.49

Brailsford

A34

5

A50

Loggerheads

Uttoxeter

Trent

S T A F F O R D S H I R E

Tutbury

Weston

Burton upon Trent

14

Stafford

A38

13

Rugeley

A449

Sherwood Pines Forest Park

MANSFIELD
Situated off B6030 east of Old
Clipstone. (SK612646)
1200HA (3,000 ACRES)
FORESTRY COMMISSION

Sherwood Pines is the East
Midlands' largest open access
wood. It is dominated, as the
name suggests, by pines with
just pockets of birch, oak and
beech. First impressions of the
site are of a well maintained
and organised woodland.

Mainly used by cyclists,
(bikes can be hired) this is a
working wood with a host of
recreational and associated
facilities and visitors are kept
well informed thanks to some
excellent interpretation and
informative maps.

There are lots of glades and
open areas throughout the
wood. Children with a sense
of adventure can explore
the site to make their own
discoveries or take part in a
programme of organised play.
You may even be lucky
enough to glimpse fallow deer
under the trees or hear rare
nightjars above the heather at
dusk.

Rufford Country Park and Abbey

OLLERTON
Located 3km (2 miles) south of
Ollerton off A614. (SK643652)
40HA (99 ACRES) SSSI
NOTTINGHAMSHIRE COUNTY COUNCIL

Woodland is just a small – but
enjoyable – part of any visit to
Rufford Country Park and
Abbey, which is popular
throughout the year, especially
in summer. However there are
plenty of tranquil spots to be
found in and around the
grounds of the former
Cistercian abbey, which now
houses a cafe, restaurant, garden
centre and arts and crafts venue
where activities take place year-
round.

Explore beyond the abbey
and its stables and you discover
an arboretum with formal gardens containing some interesting sculptures one of which –
a concrete bench framed by a
farmer with a ram – is a particular favourite with children.

Well-marked and laid paths
lead through expanses of grass
to an ornamental lake that
culminates in a weir and jetty.
The woodland, with holly and
yew and other species
associated with Sherwood

Forest is reached by well-marked, surfaced paths with points of interest highlighted.

Dukes Wood

NEWARK

Entrance to reserve is off minor road to Eakring, which leaves the A617 near Kirklington. (SK675603)

8HA (20 ACRES) SSSI

NOTTINGHAMSHIRE WILDLIFE TRUST

It's fascinating to think that the beautiful 20 acre reserve known as Dukes Wood stands on the site of the UK's first onshore oilfield – where some 280,000 tons of oil have been extracted.

On this unique site the area's industrial heritage can be appreciated whilst enjoying its natural heritage – for today it is a mixed deciduous woodland, part of which is a Site of Special Scientific Interest (SSSI).

Dominant trees are oak, ash, hazel and birch. Guelder rose, dogwood, wild privet and elder can be found in the shrub layer. You may be lucky enough to spot blackcap, spotted flycatcher and jays. Or hear the tapping of the great spotted woodpecker. Butterflies abound but the resident red deer, fox and stoat are rarely seen. Some of the 'nodding donkeys' – pumps that worked the oilfield – have been restored and can be seen close to a specially created industrial archaeology nature trail called the Dukes Wood Trail.

There is a small information centre documenting the history and development of the site and a leaflet describes highlights found on the trail.

A small section of the site is private.

below:
Rufford Country Park

Thieves and Harlow Woods

MANSFIELD OR KIRKBY IN ASHFIELD
Thieves Wood has two car parks off the
B6139. A third car park at Portland
Training College provides access to
Harlow Wood from A60. (SK552567)
147HA (363 ACRES)
FORESTRY COMMISSION

Now part of the Greenwood,
Thieves Wood was once part of
the Royal Wood of Lyndhurst.
Its name is thought to have
come from the activities of
highwaymen who preyed on
travellers heading north on the
King's Way.

Today it is still a hive of
activity, but the emphasis is on
walking, riding and picnicking.
The woodland boasts an array
of paths and tracks covering
undulating terrain. One of the
longer trails follows the route
of the King's Way to link the
car park with the visitor centre.
Harlow Wood is a quieter setting. The site, which surrounds
Portland Training College, is
well used by local residents for
riding, walking and exercising
their dogs and many people
enjoy a stop in the small
college tea room after a long
walk through the woods. The
site has a short surfaced route,
suitable for people needing less
able access.

Blidworth Woods

BLIDWORTH
Located west off A614 (Nottingham to
Doncaster). Woods can be accessed
from A614 along Longdale Lane.
(SK597545)
400HA (989 ACRES)
FORESTRY COMMISSION

Romantics will love the fact
that Blidworth Woods, in the
very heart of the old Royal
Forest of Sherwood, still contain echoes of their historic
origins, through its ancient
oaks and remnant heathland.

The woods include Sansom
and Haywood Oaks as well as
Blidworth and provide a variety of walks ranging from a
short surfaced trail suitable for
wheelchair users and cyclists to
longer cross-country hikes, all
offering much of interest from
ancient oaks to nightjars.

A waymarked trail linking
the three car parks allows
exploration of the woods – and
it's possible to join the Robin
Hood Way, linking Thieves
Wood beyond. Popular with
riders too, the woods provide a
horse box park at Blidworth
Bottoms car park and
waymarked bridle tracks,

Bestwood Country Park

NOTTINGHAM
Access from Park Road, off Bestwood
Road (B683) and A611 or Bestwood
Lodge Drive near B6004. (SK565474)
260HA (643 ACRES)
NOTTINGHAMSHIRE COUNTY COUNCIL
AND GEDLING BOROUGH COUNCIL

Once part of Sherwood Forest and now part of the extensive Greenwood Community Forest, Bestwood Country Park is a history-steeped site. Originally a royal hunting preserve used by a large number of English monarchs, the estate was acquired by Nell Gwynne in 1687. A medieval hunting lodge once stood on the site of the Victorian built Bestwood Lodge.

By 1939, with the golden age of English country estates over, the estate was sold off but today the 650 acres that formed the country park are a recreational magnet for thousands of people.

An array of habitats – from woodland and wetland to wild flower meadow and reedbed – hosts thousands of species and this is thought to be the county's richest site for fungi, with more than 200 species recorded. A series of guided walks, events, courses and conservation projects are organised throughout the year, though riders must have a permit.

below:
Bestwood Country Park

above:
Shipley Country Park (p.42)

Oldmoor Wood

NOTTINGHAM

Take A610 east towards Nottingham.
Turn right onto A6002 to Strelley. Park
in Strelley village and wood is accessed
down a country lane 200m north of
church. (SK499420)

15HA (38 ACRES)

THE WOODLAND TRUST

Considering Nottingham City
Centre is a mere 8km (5 miles)
away, Oldmoor Wood lies in a
surprisingly rural area, part of
an undulating landscape of
farmland, hedgerows and small
woodlands.

The wood itself is mainly flat
with an attractive combination
of high forest and open glades
with dense scrub along the
south west boundary. A
network of tracks form easy
circular walks through the
wood. There is a good variety
of trees, the dominant canopy
being oak, ash, sycamore and
beech with an understorey
including holly, rowan, blackthorn and hawthorn.

Bluebells, dense in patches,
are scattered throughout the
wood where you can also find
wood anemone, wood-sorrel,
lesser celandine and creeping
jenny. Within the wood is a
small circular pond, with beautiful old yews standing on its
central island.

Kedleston Hall, Priestwood and Vicarwood

DERBY

National Trust sign posts from A38.
(SK313404)
354HA (874 ACRES)
THE NATIONAL TRUST

Phone 01332 842191 for opening times

The approach to Priestwood and Vicarwood, along an elegant drive, provides an impressive introduction to the park, with constantly changing and panoramic views of veteran trees, roundels, lakes and a magnificent neo-classical Hall. The parkland surrounding Kedleston Hall was designed by the same man who designed the neo-classical building itself, Robert Adam.

The site's historical interest is complemented by the variety in its boundary woods, parkland with veteran oak and beech, lakes and the Pleasure Ground which was landscaped in the 1760s. A number of stately veteran oaks are scattered across the park, both in avenues and informal groups. Evidence of a ha-ha can be seen between the grassland and woodland.

The woods, populated primarily by oak, lime, beech, ash, horse chestnut and yew – and large numbers of squirrels – undergo a subtle character change where long and short walks diverge, where there is a younger plantation of pine and the occasional veteran beech and oak. Where the wood meets the lake edge there is a new beech maze. The park is open to the public between March and December.

Bramcote Hills Park Woodland

STAPLEFORD

Take Ilkeston Road (A6007) east from major roundabout on A52. Follow signs for Ilkeston for approx 800m (½ mile). Car park is on right. (SK499384)
7HA (16 ACRES)
BROXTOWE BOROUGH COUNCIL

left:
Kedleston Hall, Priestwood and Vicarwood

left:
*Shipley Country
Park*

Shipley Country Park

HEANOR
Take A608 from Heanor to Smalley.
Turn left into Heanor Gate Industrial
Park, turn right at the end leading
directly to the car park.(SK431453)
250 HA (600 ACRES)
DERBYSHIRE COUNTY COUNCIL

Created as part of a pioneering
landscape reclamation
programme by the National
Coal Board in the 1970s, Shipley
Country Park is the place to go
for variety and a busy all-year
round events calendar.

Once mines and spoil heaps,
the area has lots to offer, from
established woods, a reservoir
and wetlands to open space, a
fishing lake and the site of
Shipley Hall with its restored
formal gardens and quirky water
tower.

The information centre has a
wealth of amenities, along with a
wildlife garden and toddlers'
play area – and improvements
are constantly being made. There
are plenty of surfaced paths, but
the going can get muddy so
remember your boots.

If you prefer more tranquil,
established woodland, Shipley
Wood in the eastern corner of
the park fits the bill with oak, ash
and birch. Smaller copses can be
found along Bell Lane bridleway
to the west.

Black Rocks

CROMFORD

Take B5036 (off A6) south towards Wirksworth. After approx 1.6km (1 mile) take left hand turn signed Black Rocks. Car park 200m on left.

(SK291557)

85HA (210 ACRES)

FORESTRY COMMISSION

Black Rocks takes its name from the massive gritstone outcrops over the car park at the entrance to the site. Long popular with climbers, they also provide visitors with some impressive views across the stunning Peak District National Park.

Easy to explore, via some well marked routes, the site is dominated by conifers – Corsican and lodgepole pines – but also has areas of beech and sycamore. This area provides a good habitat for small birds such as the goldcrest. Most of the woodland trails lead through the more diverse areas of the site: glades and open areas of heather linking with more mature woodland. You can also enjoy some pleasing views across the countryside from a series of vantage points along the trails.

An interesting feature of the site is old lead mine workings, where the vivacious mountain pansy thrives on the spoil heaps.

Wheata Woods

SHEFFIELD

Follow signs for Grenoside village from A61. Head north out of village along Woodhead Road.

(SK326493)

55HA (136 ACRES)

SHEFFIELD CITY COUNCIL

Carsington Water

MATLOCK

Off B5035 between Matlock and Ashbourne, follow brown tourist signs.

(SK224527)

42HA (104 ACRES)

SEVERN TRENT WATER

Shining Cliff Woods

WIRKSWORTH

Take the Alderwasley turn off A6. Public footpath is off this road (approx 100m on right).

(SK339526)

78HA (193 ACRES) SSSI

FORESTRY COMMISSION

Bow Wood

Lea Bridge
From A6 exit at junction near
Cromford take minor road towards
Holloway. Wood is before Cromford
Mill and Holloway. Park at Lea Bridge.
(SK315564)
10HA (25 ACRES)
THE WOODLAND TRUST

Bow Wood near Matlock is a
good example of the semi-natural oak and birch woodland
that once cloaked the area. Set
on a sloping site, it faces south
and west across the Derwent
Valley. At the top of the wood
is the Wickey Tor, which offers
stunning views towards the
north east across the valley and
into the Peak District National
Park.

A quiet place, Bow Wood is
only well used by local people
and walkers using the Shining
Cliffs complex of paths. Once
inside you are likely to
discover some large beech and
sycamore. Bracken provides
most of the ground cover, with
beautiful golden colours in the
autumn. Recent clearing work
has prompted the appearance
of some young oaks. The central field allows much more
light into the wood, giving it a
very different and striking
character.

Brierley Forest Park

Sutton-in-Ashfield
Main entrance and car park on Skegby
Road, Huthwaite, near the M1/A38
junction. (SK476600)
100HA (247 ACRES)
ASHFIELD DISTRICT COUNCIL

Tue–Sun 11am–4pm in summer;
11am–3pm in winter

Nurtured as a young section of
the Greenwood Community
Forest, Brierley Forest Park
has been moulded from former
colliery land, farmland and
council playing fields into an
extensive mosaic of landscaped
habitats.

Some 80,000 trees were
planted in the mid 1990s to
effect the transformation, along
with the creation of a new lake,
wetlands and wild flower
meadows. Set on one of the
highest points in
Nottinghamshire, the site also
provides some stunning views
over the surrounding countryside.

Everyone has been catered
for at Brierley Forest.
Extensive, well marked routes
are provided for walkers,
cyclists, riders and the less
abled and there are nature conservation areas, art and
recreation facilities and a useful
visitor centre. A recent

addition to the site is a sculpture trail.

The area's rich history – linked with coal mining, railways and agriculture – adds another interesting facet to any visit.

Halldale Wood

Two Dales
A6 between Bakewell and Matlock, exit at B5057 north eastwards. At Two Dales take road to Darley Hilside. Take first right and take right at next junction. Wood is on right and can be reached via the footpath. (SK283643)
21HA (53 ACRES)
THE WOODLAND TRUST

Set atop the steeply sloping sides of a valley, Halldale Wood forms a sizeable slice of the woodland that straddles Halldale Brook. The eastern side of the valley is a good example of the oak and birch woodland that once cloaked the area and there are attractive pockets of ash along the valley floor.

The woodland itself is classed as semi-natural ancient woodland and yew, an ancient woodland indicator, helps to confirm its status. Some sections of the site were replanted between 1920 and 1973 – predominantly with mixed broadleaves.

There is a good variety of ground flora and a large variety of woodland birds to be discovered throughout the year. Visitors are advised to go prepared with stout footwear.

Greenwood Community Forest

Nottinghamshire's Community Forest, the Greenwood covers vast swathes of the county, where a working partnership is providing a greener setting close to the homes of more than a million people.

The Greenwood covers a 417km^2- (161 sq. mile-) landscape linking historic Sherwood Forest in the north east with Attenborough in the south west. The forest itself incorporates a host of smaller woods and landscapes – including Brierley Forest Park, Foxcovert Plantation, Bestwood Country Park and Burntstump Country Park along with Colliers Wood, Dob Park, Moor Pond and Dams Bank Wood, Portland Park Local Nature Reserve, Vicar Water Country Park, Bulwell Hall Park and Thieves Wood.

Coombes Valley

LEEK

Follow A523 Leek to Ashbourne. After 6.4km (4 miles) turn left, signed for Apesford and RSPB Coombes Valley. (SK009534)

160HA (395 ACRES) SSSI

RSPB

Coombes Valley is a wonderfully secluded and sheltered wooded valley that contrasts dramatically with the open, exposed landscape of the Staffordshire moorlands through which it runs.

Broadleaved woodland of oak, birch, holly and beech, runs through the valley which also features species-rich streamside meadows. Up on the higher ground there are open areas of heather, with bracken and gorse, enclosed by old drystone walls. Along the top of the valley are areas of young broadleaved woodland, which contrast with the adjacent mature woodland.

Small birds favour the woodland edges and two hides, one overlooking a pond and the other in the tree tops, provide the chance to stop and watch for woodpeckers and the herons that feed at the pond and along the stream.

Castern Wood

LEEK

From village of Ilam take the minor road towards Wetton. Follow road through Stanshope to T-junction at Hopedale. Turn left, 500m (⅓ mile) turn left, 500m (⅓ mile) park on right. (SK120538)

21HA (51 ACRES) AONB SSSI

STAFFORDSHIRE WILDLIFE TRUST

Castern Wood, part of the stunning Peak District, is arguably one of the country's finest and most scenic reserves. The site is part of the Hamps and Manifold Valley Site of Special Scientific Interest (SSSI) within the Peak District Dales area, recently designated as a Special Area of Conservation, recognising its status at European level.

The reserve has a diverse range of deciduous woodland – dominated by oak, ash, hazel and field maple. Small and large-leaved lime are present indicating the antiquity of the woodland. Over 340 species of plant have been recorded including – spring flowering cowslips and violets followed by orchids and aromatic salad burnet. In the valley meadow along the river you may find the pinkish nodding heads of water avens which are common along the banks in summer.

The meandering course of the River Manifold forms the western boundary. During dry spells the river vanishes, flowing underground and reappearing further downstream at Ilam.

Excellent views can be enjoyed, particularly across the Manifold Valley and Beeston Tor and the site has an interesting historical aspect. The valley was mined for lead during the 19th century and several tunnels remain within the reserve.

Dovedale

ASHBOURNE
Brown tourist sign on A515 just north of Ashbourne. Car park between Thorpe and Ilam, follow signs to Dovedale. (SK145520)
123HA (304 ACRES) AONB SSSI
THE NATIONAL TRUST

Clear waters running through a deep limestone gorge, dramatic Peak District scenery, rocky outcrops and varied woodland... it's not surprising Dovedale is a people magnet. Such is the impact of its popularity that the National Trust does not actively encourage more visitors, but out of season, there is a better opportunity to explore.

The River Dove provides the focus throughout an exciting and varied walk. Dippers are common, crayfish less so. Spectacular limestone outcrops add drama and some have names – Twelve Apostles, Lover's Leap and Dovedale Church. Caves along the eastern side of the valley delight young visitors.

Within the woodland are rowan, whitebeam, field maple – and yew which grows on the rocky outcrops – along with a distinctive assemblage of plants, including dog's mercury and burnet rose. Grassland areas along the valley support a host of birds and butterflies.

below: *Jacob's Ladder, Dovedale*

above:
Harston Wood

Harston Wood

CHEADLE
Take A52 from Froghall towards
Ashbourne and almost immediately
turn left to Foxt. Parking 400m (¼ mile)
on County Council car park/picnic site.
Follow footpath to reserve boundary.
(SK034479)
18HA (45 ACRES) SSSI
STAFFORDSHIRE WILDLIFE TRUST

Part of the largest remaining concentration of woodland in Staffordshire, Harston Wood sustains a wonderful variety of wildlife. Most of the woodland is dominated by ash along with elm, though alder car predominates along the valley bottom.

Redstart, wood warbler and pied flycatcher have been recorded in the wood along with great and lesser spotted woodpecker, nuthatch, treecreeper, long-tailed tits and tawny owl.

Ground flora in the valley bottom includes the rare opposite-leaved golden-saxifrage, great horsetail and marsh-marigolds while late spring brings the white flowers and aroma of wild garlic which grows in abundance.

Many woods in the area used to be managed by coppicing but there is no history of coppicing here for 80 years and there are large numbers of dead and mature trees supporting a rich invertebrate population.

Cotton Dell

CHEADLE

Take B5417 from Cheadle towards
Oakamoor. County Council car park on
right indicated from road as you enter
Oakamoor (SK054449)

64HA (158 ACRES)

STAFFORDSHIRE WILDLIFE TRUST

Cotton Dell, an area of ancient woodland in the Churnet Valley, is home to a number of unusual species. The varied woodland of ash, oak, hazel and elm includes less common species such as guelder rose, field maple and bird cherry while tall alders thrive in wetter spots at the base of the valley. Wild flowers are abundant, with bluebells, wood-sorrel, wood anemone and the uncommon greater woodrush.

Winding through the reserve is the Cotton Brook Stream, important for its dramatic rock exposures, and dippers and grey wagtails can often be seen along the bank of the stream. Plants that prefer damp habitats – for example golden saxifrage and water avens, can be discovered here.

Large numbers of birds live on the reserve, including all three native species of woodpecker, chiffchaff, warblers and nuthatch.

Dimmings Dale

CHEADLE

From Cheadle take B5417 to Oakamoor
village, turn right at bottom of steep hill
before bridge in village. Take first left
and follow narrow lane towards Alton.
Car park is on left by Ramblers Retreat
Cafe. (SK064434)

260HA (643 ACRES) SSSI

FORESTRY COMMISSION

Dimmings Dale is a spacious ancient woodland site cloaking the sides of the Churnet Valley. In spring the slopes become a misty carpet of bluebells, wood anemones and wood-sorrel while purple foxgloves tower among ferns and bilberries.

The area has a rich industrial heritage and ore smelting flourished here for 150 years. What was once littered with spoil heaps has developed into a photographer's dream. Scots pine tower above huge rock outcrops, forged in the Ice Age and offering natural resting places along the route of the walk, while large ponds strung along a sparkling stream make a necklace decorating the valley floor. These form part of a Site of Special Scientific Interest (SSSI) through the dale.

Newcastle-under-Lyme

Stoke-on-Trent

Ashbourne

Cheadle

Brailsford

A524

A5

A50

Loggerheads

Uttoxeter

Trent

A34

STAFFORDSHIRE

Tutbury

Forem
Wo

Weston

Burton
upon Trent

14

Stafford

Battlestead Hill p.53

Top Wood, Long Close Woo
and Toptree Wood p.5

13

Rugeley

Cannock
Chase p.54

Roxliston Forestry Centre p.55

A38

Coton
Wood p.55

A449

Pipe Hall Farm p.55

Grangewood Farm Fo

A5

12

Cannock

Church Gresley Wood

Lichfield

Donisthor
Woodland Park p.

11

A5

Temple Wood

2 1

Brownhills

Tamworth

10

M6

Walsall

WEST

M42

Wolverhampton

10

9

9

West
Bromwich

8 7

Dudley

1

6

5

4A

8

2

Stourbridge

BIRMINGHAM

4

Halesowen

3

MIDLANDS

6

Kidderminster

Solihull

M42

5

A41

4

elper

Heanor

Eastwood

Arnold

Trent

A46

Nottingham

Bingham

Ilkeston

A38

A52

Derby

A52

A6005

A25

A606

DERBY CITY

Long Eaton

A50

Castle Donnington

A24

Kegworth

A60

A453

Bunny Old Wood *p.52*

A6006

oir

A52

Ticknall

Cuckoo Gap Woodlands *p.63*

23A

M1

Martin's Wood *p.56*

A6

Shepshed

A512

New Lount tue Reserve *p.57*

Charley Woods *p.58*

23

Loughborough

A46

Outwoods, The *p.58*

Sarah's Wood *p.54*

Beacon Hill Country Park *p.60*

Willesley New Woods *p.56*

A47

Coalville

Mountsorrel

Swithland Wood *p.62*

Syston

Willesley Woodland *p.59*

22

Birstall

Ibstock

22A

Sheet Hedges Wood *p.65*

ce Valley Park *p.62*

Battram Wood *p.66*

21A

Martinshaw Wood *p.64*

Leicester

A444

Royal Tigers and Centenary Wood *p.66*

Old Woodlands Farm *p.65*

LEICESTER CITY

Bagworth Heath Woods *p.66*

21

Wigston

Burroughs Wood *p.67*

Earl Shilton

M69

Oadby

A5

L E I C E S T E R S H I R E

Hinckley

2

Nuneaton

1

A426

A5199

3

2

Lutterworth

20

Husbands Bosworth

Coventry

A428

A4304

A14

1

19

Rugby

A5199

Bunny Old Wood

KEYWORTH
Main entrance on Bunny Hill off A60
Loughborough road. (SK579283)
16HA (40 ACRES)
NOTTINGHAMSHIRE WILDLIFE TRUST

Bunny Old Wood is an ancient coppiced woodland with a varied and interesting history.

The site, which is mentioned in the Domesday Book, once provided timber for Saxon settlers. Henry VII and his army camped nearby en route for the Battle of East Stoke. Historical evidence of the wood's age takes the form of ancient ditches running along the northern and southern edges and old coppice stools. Coppiced ash and field maple are a common sight while the southern boundary includes oak, cherry and wild crab apple, along with wood anemone, stitchwort and barren strawberry.

It's rich in wildlife – more than 50 species of bird have been recorded, including the great and lesser spotted woodpecker and more than 20 butterfly species seen here include the white letter hairstreak. Some of the dead timber has been retained to encourage woodpeckers while habitat piles have been built for small mammals, invertebrates and fungi.

Foremark Reservoir Woodlands

SWADLINCOTE
From A514 at Ticknall take signposted turn at end of village. (SK337245)
51HA (126 ACRES) SSSI
SEVERN TRENT WATER

Woodland exploration is one of a host of activities you can undertake on a visit to Foremark Reservoir, including visiting Carves Rocks a Site of Special Scientific Interest (SSSI).

The reservoir area, which contains a number of interesting wildlife habitats, also offers the chance to fish, birdwatch, sail or cycle. But for those who love woodland, the real joy is in exploration and discovering the magic of the growing National Forest.

The woodland, which stands east of the reservoir, was planted in the 1970s with mainly native species as part of a long-term plan to encourage wildlife conservation and expand amenities. Most of the wood has been planted with oak, rowan, holly and silver birch.

There is some 22 acres of community woodland, with surfaced footpaths concentrated around the visitor centre. The remainder of the site has steep gradients in places.

Battlestead Hill

TATENHILL
From A38 at Burton-on-Trent take junction to Tatenhill. Track leading to wood is off first left hand bend immediately after leaving A38. (SK208221)
2HA (6 ACRES)
THE WOODLAND TRUST

Battlestead Hill wood is an important landscape feature within the Tatenhill Conservation Area. Mainly mature woodland with grassland and scrub lying in a narrow valley, the site is sandwiched between two new broadleaf planting schemes – the 70 acre Bass Millennium Wood to the north east and East Hill Wood, a 45 acre site, to the west.

The woodland mix includes mature beech, English oak, ash, sycamore and wild cherry while bramble dominates the ground flora. You will also find marsh thistle favouring the rides and open areas.

A network of rides and paths links Battlestead with its fledgling neighbours and a well used public footpath bisects the wood along the main ride. A circular footpath in the archaeologically interesting south east corner of the wood is very steep in places and can be hard going – particularly in the wet. This area houses earthworks – a series of banks and gullies – believed to be medieval or even earlier in origin.

below:
Battlestead Hill

Cannock Chase

STAFFORD OR RUGELY

Take A51 through Rugely. Turn into
Hagley road at traffic lights between the
two roundabouts signposted to
Cannock Chase visitor centre.
(SK017171)
65KM2 (25 SQ. MILES) AONB
FORESTRY COMMISSION

Cannock Chase is Britain's
smallest mainland Area of
Outstanding Natural Beauty
(AONB), an area of about
65km² (25 sq. miles) of rolling
hills covered with lowland
heaths and mixed forests. The
varied landscape provides a
stunning contrast between the
autumn colours of the forests
and the purple heathland.

This area has rich environ-
mental and historical interest
– it was once a royal hunting
preserve for the Bishops of
Lichfield. During the 16th
century the woodland was cut
for charcoal burning. Long
associated with the armed
forces, it was also the site of
the country's first ever large
scale military manoeuvres in
1872.

There are a large number of
attractions, among them
museums, family cycle routes
and a herd of fallow deer.

Many visitors like to start
out from the Birches Valley
Forest Centre, where there is
an excellent shop and an edu-
cation team.

Sarah's Wood

MOIRA

Take Measham turn off on A42. Turn
right onto B586 to Donisthorpe. Carry
on to Moira. Car park is 250m north of
Moira crossroads. (SK315158)
12HA (30 ACRES)
LEICESTERSHIRE COUNTY COUNCIL

Designed by – and for – the
less abled, Sarah's Wood
stands in the heart of the
National Forest close to the
impressive National Forest
and Conkers exhibition
centres.

The paths, a combination of
tarmac and finely crushed
stone, provide good access for
wheelchair users (though
assistance is needed in some
sections) and interpretation is
provided at wheelchair level,
where the edges of shrubs
have been cut back to display
the twig colours of species
such as willows and
dogwoods. A play area,
suitable for the less able, is
also provided. Panoramic
views can be enjoyed of the
developing local landscapes.

Below the wood sits the canal basin, which links with the Ashby canal and this can be accessed by less-abled visitors from the car park at the National Forest Centre.

Rosliston Forestry Centre

BARTON UNDER NEEDWOOD
Take A38 south from Derby, exit at Burton-under-Needwood. Take road to Walton-on-Trent and then Rosliston village, at T-junction turn left and centre is on right. (SK241172)
64HA (158 ACRES)
FORESTRY COMMISSION

Grangewood Farm Forest

DONISTHORPE
A444 at Overseal take minor road west signposted Coton in the Elms, Lullington. After approx 1.6km (1 mile) turn right to Grangewood Hall, car park is further 2.4km (11/2 miles) on right. (SK273142)
40HA (99 ACRES)
MR KIRKLAND

Pipe Hall Farm

BURNTWOOD
From A461 between Lichfield and Brownhills, take A1590 west towards Burntwood. Take road towards Woodhouses, turn right in the village and car park is approx 400m (¼ mile) on the right. (SK083095)
49HA (120 ACRES)
THE WOODLAND TRUST

Top Wood, Long Close Wood and Toptree Wood

BURTON-ON TRENT
Leave A444 travelling west towards Linton. At T-junction, turn left and left at fork in road. Wood is on left hand side half way down this road. (SK270155)
81HA (200 ACRES)
THE WOODLAND TRUST

Coton Wood

BURTON-ON-TRENT
Turn west off A444 at Overseal, towards Coton in the Elms. In village take Little Liverpool Road. Wood is off this road to left. (SK245145)
33HA (82 ACRES)
THE WOODLAND TRUST

Willesley New Woods

ASHBY DE LA ZOUCH

From Ashby de la Zouch take B5003 Moira road. At Norris Hill, turn onto Willesley Woodside. Wood is approx 1.6km (1 mile) along Willesley Woodside. (SK329156)

24HA (60 ACRES)

UK COAL MINING LTD

Some of the first trees in the National Forest are said to have been planted at Willesley Wood. There are two distinct areas of planting within Willesley: the 1990 plantation and more recent planting of alder, ash, birch and oak. This is a good place to enjoy the surrounding countryside.

Wide rides and open areas at the crest of the hill will create new habitats as the wood matures and some areas are already being colonised by flora and fauna.

Nearby Shellbrook Wood is a newer site, with planting dating from 1998. Part of the site is dominated by an open cast coalface and railhead, an industrial memento that reminds us this is a developing landscape. This wood links with a footpath to Ashby and adjacent new planting at Chestnut Wood.

The site can be a challenge to explore. An interpretation board in the car park would be useful to steer visitors towards the circular walk within the wood.

Martin's Wood

WOODHOUSE EAVES

Exit M1 at junction 23. Take A412 west and exit at B591. Follow road to crossroad and continue straight on. Take the next left onto Deans Lane and the wood is on right at top of the hill. (SK507152)

5HA (12 ACRES)

THE WOODLAND TRUST

Martin's Wood in Charnwood Forest stands among the Midland's highest woodland, offering spectacular views across the Soar and Trent valleys. Named after the late president of the Friends of Charnwood, the site was originally gently sloping grassland with two shelterbelts of oak, beech, holly, sycamore and rowan, encompassed by drystone walls characteristic of the area.

In 1995 the Woodland Trust supplemented this with a programme of planting – with oak, ash, birch, field maple and a variety of shrubs. An open area of grassland was retained and this is mown for hay in July to encourage a rich mixture of wild grasses and flowers.

Access is provided by a network of paths and rides that provides a circular route, taking in two main vantage points. A public bridleway running alongside the wood gives easy access to Beacon Hill Country Park.

New Lount Nature Reserve

Shepshed

Take A512 east from Ashby-de-la-Zouch junction of A42 then first left on B5324 towards Belton. Take B587 to Melbourne. Entrance is left. (SK399185)

20ha (49 acres)

Leicestershire County Council

After more than 30 years as a colliery, a former tip is re-emerging as New Lount Nature Reserve, a vibrant landscape where wildlife habitats are evolving. Popular with local youngsters, it encompasses fragments of ancient woodland with oak, ash and birch and in the wetter parts, alder and willow.

Approached from the site of the old mine entrance the reserve is served by bridleways and footpaths, while a circular walk follows the line of the old narrow-gauge rail line that once transported coal around the site. Birch and gorse are colonising the bare ground on its route.

You might spot a woodpecker, tree creeper, goldcrest or chiffchaff. Flowers include orchids, scabious, trefoil, stonecrop, vipers bugloss and St. Johns Wort. Around the ponds you can find frogs, moorhen, dragonflies and damselflies. The paths here can get muddy – so stout shoes are recommended.

Church Gresley Wood

Swadlincote

From A444 Overseal, turn onto Park Road. 400m (¼ mile) on left take A511 Woodville to Albert village. Park in Occupation Road on right. (SK293171)

41ha (101acres)

Tapton Estates

The Outwoods

LOUGHBOROUGH
Take A512 from Loughborough. Turn left down Snell's Nook lane and straight at the Priory traffic lights. Follow Woodhouse lane for 1.6km (1 mile). The car park is on left. (SK515160)
45HA (110 ACRES) SSSI
CHARNWOOD BOROUGH COUNCIL

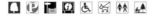

The evocatively named Outwoods has something of a fairytale quality. Once part of Charnwood Forest, its rocky outcrops, some lent an orange luminosity by lichen, are unique to this area, hence its Site of Special Scientific Interest (SSSI) status.

At every twist and turn of the woodland, there is something to discover – rare plants, including heath rush and tall sedge, for example – as you are drawn to the centre of the site, which has been wooded for centuries. Indeed, records date back to 500AD.

Its eastern boundary features a cluster of the ancient oaks that once dominated the forest. Today there is also pine, spruce and larch and younger blocks of oak. Look out for a plaque, unveiled by the Prince of Wales, commemorating the work of Dr Richard St Barbe Baker who founded 'Men of the Trees'. The woodland paths are well surfaced and benches are dotted about the site.

Charley Woods

WHITWICK
Approx 1.6km (1 mile) north west of Copt Oak off the A511. Access to reserve along track which leaves the Whitwick Road opposite Upper Greenhill Farm. (SK476148)
67HA (165 ACRES)
LEICS AND RUTLAND WILDLIFE TRUST

Named after nearby Charley Hall, Charley Woods is actually made up of three separate areas, Burrow Wood, Field Wood and Cat Hill Wood, linked by public footpaths. Burrow Wood is open, with views of Timberwood Hill to the west. It is dominated by oak, with birch, rowan and ash, hazel and guelder rose. A series of springs and a stream run alongside a track, marked by a thriving line of holly.

The field area has been left to regenerate naturally and oak and birch are already emerging. A pond has been created in the north east corner and natural wetlands lie in the south east. Wild flowers such as lady's smock do well in the wetter area and higher up the hill are gorse and broom.

above:
Willesley Woodland

Cat Hill Wood has a subtly different feel, with a dense understorey of thorn and holly.

Willesley Woodland

ASHBY DE LA ZOUCH

Leave A42 at B5006 junction signposted for Ashby de la Zouch. After approx 1.6km (1 mile) turn sharp left, sign posted to Donisthorpe. Follow road for 2.4km (1½ miles). At small cross roads turn left into Willesley Woodland. (SK335142)

40HA (99 ACRES)

THE WOODLAND TRUST

You will discover Willesley Woodland next to the village of Donisthorpe, in the heart of the National Forest. The wood is one of the first to evolve within Leicestershire's coalfield. When mining ended in 1943 the land was returned to agricultural use but its industrial heritage is never far from view, with visible relics including nearby Oakthorpe Colliery. Subsidence flash evident as a lake within the boundaries of the woodland site.

With new and mature woods, wetlands, wild-flower meadows and the rare majestic black poplar, over 70 different types of bird have made Willesley Woodland their home. There are even ancient woodland indicators such as bluebells and dog's mercury. This award-winning woodland creation site is one of 20 Woodland Trust properties in the National Forest.

Beacon Hill Country Park

WOODHOUSE EAVES
Situated 14.5km (9 miles) north of
Leicester and 3km (2 miles) south of
Loughborough on outskirts of
Woodhouse Eaves. Entrance on
Breakback Road, off Beacon Road.
(SK520149)
135HA (334 ACRES) SSSI
LEICESTERSHIRE COUNTY COUNCIL

Not only is Beacon Hill Country Park widely recognised as an ecological and archaeological gem, but the 244m- (800ft-) high summit of Beacon Hill is Leicestershire's second highest point, offering panoramic views of the county. The park, owned and managed by Leicestershire County Council, is a huge draw for visitors. Seats placed around the park allow visitors to relax and enjoy the scenery and some of these seats, made from silver birch trunks, also provide a winter home for small mammals.

The site is made up of mixed woodland, heathland, grassland and farmland. Before and during the Second World War many of the larger trees were lost but specimens of beech, sweet chestnut and Scots pine remain along with native oak and silver birch. A native tree collection has been established close to one of the car parks – the track here is suitable for less abled access – through a planting programme of around 8,000 trees. The collection represents 28 species of tree which became naturally established in Britain after the last Ice Age.

An area of open heathland around the slopes provides an invaluable wildlife habitat and a special programme of nocturnal walks provides the chance to glimpse a fox, tawny owl or one of five types of bat inhabiting the woodland. If you are lucky you may spot a badger hunting for grubs along the woodland edge. The site's ecological importance is reflected in the fact that much of it is designated a Site of Special Scientific Interest (SSSI).

Historically this is a fascinating place to visit, too. Evidence of prehistoric life can be seen through a series of earthworks, the remains of a hillfort dating back as much as 3,000 years to the Bronze Age. Bronze bracelets, axe moulds and spearheads have been discovered on the Beacon Hill, a scheduled ancient monument.

above left:
Beacon Hill Country Park

above:
Beacon Hill Country Park

Sence Valley Forest Park

Ibstock
Take A447 north from Ibstock. Main entrance is on left approx 800m (½ mile) north of village. (SK404113)
60HA (148 ACRES)
FORESTRY COMMISSION

Part community forest, part country park, Sence Valley Forest Park is a spectacular example of a dynamic evolving landscape and shows how good design can transform derelict land into a natural asset.

The woodland is tucked away off the Ravenstone Road north of Ibstock and it is not until you leave your car and walk towards the entrance that the impact of the project hits home. It is then that the breathtaking view of the valley below opens up to you.

The network of paths enables walkers, cyclists and riders alike to get the most from the valley without posing a risk to nesting birds. The paths are suitable for pushchairs and the rustic sculptures encountered en route are a delight to young visitors as well as old. That's not surprising, as children were involved in the woodland design, including the zigzag path that leads up the steepest gradient.

Swithland Wood

Newton Linford
Access off the B5330 and from Woodhouse Eaves. (SK538118)
59HA (146 ACRES) SSSI
BRADGATE PARK TRUST

You will discover Swithland Wood in the very heart of ancient Charnwood Forest and not surprisingly, there is an ancient 'feel' to the site. For example a rocky cove inside the wood looks like something straight out of a fantasy tale. The pool is fenced off most of the time but occasionally used by divers. Rocky outcrops make it an impressive sight any time of the year.

Extensive yet inviting – and very busy at weekends – the woods are mainly oak, birch and hazel interspersed with the occasional small-leaved lime and areas veer from dense woodland through dappled shade to open conditions – with a few surprises along the way. It was awarded Site of Special Scientific Interest (SSSI) status as the best remaining example of original oakwood in the Charnwood Forest.

A number of alder-lined streams run through Swithland, adding to the interest of the site. There are also a number of unusual hillocks and pits in the wood that hint at the quarrying that once took place here.

Donisthorpe Woodland Park

DONISTHORPE

From A42 take B5006 to Measham. Turn right before town centre onto B586 to Donisthorpe. Moira road car park is 250m on right after crossroads. (SK320143)

30HA (74 ACRES)

LEICESTERSHIRE COUNTY COUNCIL

The phrase 'multi-purpose forestry' acquires real meaning on a visit to Donisthorpe Woodland Park, a site that's a delight for adults – and for kids.

First planted in 1996 on a reclaimed colliery tip, some skilled land profiling on the site has reaped spectacular results: snaking paths, steep enough to be interesting without precluding access for the less abled, offer views which open out impressively. Add the atmosphere of boats on the former Ashby canal, currently being redeveloped, and the result is magic. Plans for the woodland have a strong educational element, linking in neatly with the National Forest and Conkers exhibition centres.

Well-surfaced paths provide good access throughout the site and form a seamless walk through to the Moira Forge and tea rooms.

Cuckoo Gap Woodlands

COALVILLE

Take A511 towards Leicester. Take A447 junction heading into Swannington. Take right past Robin Hood public house, wood is half way up hill on right. (SK417147)

35HA (87 ACRES)

MR ADCOCK

left:
*Martinshaw
Wood*

Martinshaw Wood

GROBY OR RATBY
Turn off A46 at junction A50 and take
turning for Groby, follow signs towards
Ratby. At first mini roundabout after
entering Ratby turn right onto
Markfield road. The car park is approx
400m on right. (SK510073)
103HA (255 ACRES)
THE WOODLAND TRUST

The ancient woodland site of
Martinshaw Wood on the edge
of the National Forest features
a variety of species, though
much of its native sessile oak
was replaced with conifers
during the 1950s. The
Woodland Trust, which
acquired the site in 1963, has
the long-term aim of returning
the site to broadleaved woodland.

The Toothills, a pre-
Cambrian rock outcrop on the
northern boundary, has
retained many of the plants
associated with ancient semi-
natural woodlands –
helleborine, primrose, wood
anemone, wood-sorrel and
sanicle. Martinshaw is also one
of the only areas in
Leicestershire containing lily-
of-the-valley.

Plans for horse and cycle
access are in the pipeline.

Old Woodlands Farm

RATBY OR DESFORD

Follow A47 east for Earl Shilton. After approx 2.4km (1½) miles take B582 sign-posted for Desford. On approach to Desford take B5380 turn off opposite college. Hollow Oak Woods is adjacent to Woodlands Farm. (SK495052)

10HA (25 ACRES)

MR F HOWITT

Old Woodlands Farm and its neighbour, Hollow Oak Woods are two new sites forming part of the National Forest. The younger of the two, Old Woodlands, has some well defined rides leading through the site, which is framed by mature hedgerows and a boundary of ash and oak.

Hollow Oak Wood, is entered from a well used and shrub-filled hedge, rich in holly, which has been allowed to develop as dense cover for wildlife. From here you can enjoy excellent views of Ratby Burrows, an ancient oak and lime woodland with remnants of a medieval embankment.

West of the wood, the Woodland Trust has undertaken its own National Forest planting scheme and in time the combined site will develop into a wonderful and well managed woodland.

Sheet Hedges Wood

ANSTEY

Entrance on Newton Linford Lane, off A50 Groby Road. (SK523081)

30HA (75 ACRES) SSSI

LEICESTERSHIRE COUNTY COUNCIL

Car park open at weekends only. Wood open at weekends only during winter

Two distinct sections make up Sheet Hedges Wood. The first is regenerating broadleaved woodland resulting from conifer thinning; the second an ancient woodland with Site of Special Scientific Interest (SSSI) status – a good habitat for plants, insects and birds.

Marked by a retained fringe of conifers and ash, the first section is a good example of vigorous natural regeneration. Emerging birch, ash, sallow, thorn and hazel are supplemented by planted oak and ash.

An arable field divides the first woodland section from its neighbouring site. Here the woodland is oak, ash and hazel with holly, complemented by regenerating birch, rowan, field maple and cherry.

Traditional management methods have been introduced in sections of the wood and you might see evidence of coppicing.

Bagworth Heath Woods

COALVILLE
Take B585 south from Coalville through Bagworth village continuing towards Merrylees. Car park is on left immediately past lakes. (SK456068)
75HA (185 ACRES)
LEICESTERSHIRE COUNTY COUNCIL

There is an excellent opportunity to see a landscape in the process of development at Bagworth Heath Woods, a large newly planted woodland on the site of a former colliery.

The wood is easy to explore, via a track leading north and a well-surfaced circular path to the south. This gentler southern route leads to an area where you can view drystone walling (from local stone), pollarding and a sculpture. A Forestry Commission demonstration area forms part of the site.

Heading north on the site you'll discover a series of ponds, laid out for fishing, with a pair of resident swans. The central island is topped with the old pit wheel.

Beyond it are patches of open ground (good for skylarks) dotted with pockets of woodland. Oak and ash are being planted on the fertile arable soils. Pine, alder, maple and poplar in less fertile areas.

Battram Wood

COALVILLE OR IBSTOCK
From B585 Coalville to Bagworth Road, turn west for Nailstone and west again for Battram. Go through village, through roadgate to car park. (SK426094)
48HA (119 ACRES)
THE ROYAL FORESTRY SOCIETY

Royal Tigers and Centenary Wood

BAGWORTH
After Ibstock take B582, and take minor road towards Bagworth. Follow the road through Bagworth, the wood is on right. (SK454070)
34HA (85 ACRES)
THE WOODLAND TRUST

Temple Wood

BOURNE
A15 north of Bourne, take road through Aslackby village; road narrows almost to a track and entrance to wood is on left after 3km (2 miles). (SK286058)
240HA (593 ACRES)

FORESTRY COMMISSION

above:
Burroughs Wood

Burroughs Wood

RATBY

From A46 follow signs for Ratby and Groby. After entering Ratby take right turn into Burroughs Lane. Wood is 800m (½ mile) on right. (SK492062)

37HA (91 ACRES)

THE WOODLAND TRUST

Burroughs Wood is a 'wood of two halves', both of them large sites and linked via a public right of way.

The northern section is a broadleaved woodland with ancient origins, proving a draw in the spring when the woodland floor is awash with a sea of bluebells. South of this is a newly planted woodland, created in 1996 and 1997, with native broadleaf species such as silver birch with its distinctive white bark and pale green leaves, and Hawthorn whose heavily scented flowers appear in May and early June. There are also remnant hedgerows and open meadows which are cut annually for hay – good news for increasing the range of flora and fauna of the area.

This is a well used site, particularly along the public and permissive bridleways. Getting around is easy, with gentle and undulating slopes.

Crowle

Scunthorpe

NORTH EAST LINCOLNSHIRE

Grimsby

Cleethorpes

Brigg

Laceby

Tetney

North Somerc

Epworth

Laughton Forest p.86

Owlet Plantation p.86

Blyton

Caistor

Binbrook

Market Rasen

Willingham Woods p.84

Louth

Mablethorp

Beckingham

Gainsborough

Wickenby Wood p.85

Eeanor Wood and Lynwode Wood p.85

Maltby le Marsh

Retford (East Retford)

Great West Wood p.81

Wragby

Rigsby Wood p.86

Alf

Newball Wood p.80

Hardy Gang Wood p.81

Saxilby

Chambers Farm Wood p.78

Horncastle

Partney

Old Wood p.82

Tuxford

Lincoln

College Wood p.78

New Park Wood p.79

Burgh le Marsh

Southrey Wood p.75

Waddington

Stapleford Wood p.74

Pinewoods, The p.77

Ostlers Plantation p.77

Tattershall Carrs p.76

Billinghay

Coningsby

Newark-on-Trent

Leadenham

LINCOLNSHIRE

Wran

Balderton High Wood p.74

Long Bennington

Leasingham

Sleaford

Heckington

Sibsey

Boston

Bingham

Grantham

Londonthorpe Wood and Alma Park p.75

Swineshead

Sutterton

Th Wa

Callans Lane Wood p.72

Gosberton

Spalding

Holbeach

Twyfords Wood p.72

Colsterworth

Morton

Pinchbeck

Sutton Bridge

Melton Mowbray

Bourne

Bourne Wood p.70

Cottesmore

Morkery Wood p.73

RUTLAND

Market Deeping

Wisbech

eek, The p.69

Oakham

Stamford

Glinton

Eye

Outwe

Lord Morton's Covert p.69

Uppingham

Peterborough

LEICESTERSHIRE

Rockingham

Whittlesey

Marc

Market Harborough

Corby

Wimblington

Chatteris

Ramsey

Rothwell

Geddington

Oundle

A1(M)

CAMBRIDGESHIRE

Kettering

Thrapston

Warboys

Sutton

Earith

Stretha

right:
The Seek

The Seek

OAKHAM
Follow the A606 through Oakham and take left turn immediately after railway crossing. Take road signposted Braunston. The wood is approx 3.2km (1½ miles) on left. (SK839073)
11HA (27 ACRES)
THE WOODLAND TRUST

Set in a prominent position on the edge of Braunston-in-Rutland and less than 3km (2 miles) from Rutland Water, The Seek has much to offer, not least some stunning panoramic views across beautiful countryside. This young woodland occupies a prominent south east slope planted between 1992 and 1994 with oak, ash and hazel.

Local school children were invited to put forward ideas for the design of the woodland, which was appropriately named The Seek, because it is the local name for a 'field running down to a stream.' It has good parking facilities in a layby beside the main entrance.

Development of the woodland is being monitored by the Rutland Natural History Society who have already recorded 20 species of butterfly, 95 species of moth and 64 bird species on the site.

Lord Morton's Covert

LEICESTER
Take A47 eastwards from Leicester, turning onto B6047 after Billesdon. Travel towards Tilton-on-the- Hill taking left onto minor road 400m (¼ mile) before entering village. After 400 (¼ mile), right turn onto Sludge Hall Hill. Woodland is on right. (SK723053)
4HA (10 ACRES)
THE WOODLAND TRUST

Bourne Wood

BOURNE

Follow A151 Corby Glen Road from Bourne. Pass the A6121 turning and entrance to Wood is 200m on right.

(TF076201)

171HA (423 ACRES)

FORESTRY COMMISSION

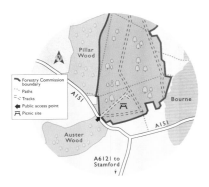

There's a magical touch about Bourne Wood, an expansive ancient woodland site that won a Forestry Centre of Excellence Award. One of its delights is a sculpture trail, full of surprises ranging from the monumental to the miniature.

A working woodland with a host of interesting facets, Bourne is easy to reach and easy to enjoy, thanks to a generous sized car park, good access, well planned facilities and a busy summer events programme. Children can make the most of a well-planned play area.

There is a dog walking trail and access for the less abled leading directly from the car park into the wood, where it is possible to spend hours exploring along the well-surfaced rides.

The site is a patchwork of differing forestry compartments, ranging from coppiced hazel to mature conifers and open grassland. The more determined walker can leave the crowds behind and head for the quieter, remote corners of the wood. The grassland habitats offer a wonderful vantage point for watching butterflies and there are extensive ponds – well worth a visit.

left:
Bourne Wood

right:
Bourne Wood

above:
Callans Lane Wood

Callans Lane Wood

BOURNE
Leave A15 Bourne to Sleaford road at
crossroads for Kirkby Underwood. Pass
through Kirkby Underwood village and
wood is on left. (TF062271)
59HA (145 ACRES)
FORESTRY COMMISSION

If you are looking for a
peaceful place for quiet
enjoyment, you'd do well to
visit Callans Lane Wood,
popular among local

residents, particularly at
weekends. A walk along the
800m (½ mile) long main ride
illustrates how work is
currently underway to
convert the site from conifers,
as they reach maturity, to
broadleaved woodland.

History enthusiasts might
already be aware that the
Roman road King Street runs
along the boundary. Indeed
the ditch and bank system
evident at the woodland
edges is a pointer to the
wood's ancient origin. Other
indications are the well-estab-
lished shrubs and veteran
trees that teem with life in the
spring. Visit at dawn or at
dusk for the chance of
spotting deer.

Access is via the long,
stony ride which eventually
forks off and paths lead
around the boundary for the
return journey. Tackle these
with stout shoes – they can
get muddy.

Twyford Woods

BOURNE
Take A151 at Colsterworth, signposted
Corby Glen and Bourne. Entrance is on
right after approx 800m (½ mile).
(SK946239)
110HA (272 ACRES)
FORESTRY COMMISSION

You'll find something of interest year-round at Twyford Woods, even though its proximity to the A1 means it's not the quietest of woods to relax in.

Great as a 'breath of air' for road travellers, it offers a variety of habitats to explore, from mixed woodland and rough grassland to scrub and wet areas. Well surfaced tracks and rides provide good access for cyclists and a network of minor paths provide a good chance to discover the woodland corners.

Many of the conifers are steadily being removed, prompting a gradual return to broadleaved woodland with strong evidence that ash, birch and willows are regenerating naturally.

The more open areas offer a good display of marsh and early-purple orchids, while primroses thrive on the ride edges.

Morkery Wood

BOURNE

From A1 take South Witham turning, then follow signs to Castle Bytham. Entrance to car park on right after 2.4km (1½ miles). (SK954192)

157HA (388 ACRES)

FORESTRY COMMISSION

Morkery Wood is a welcoming and varied wood – and a great place to witness the resurgence of native broadleaf woodland.

Birch, oak, ash and hazel are becoming re-established in the heart of the wood following the removal of conifers. Stand atop the ridge for great views but be aware of continuing extraction work – and heed any warning notices.

Beside an asphalt ride from the car park to the centre of the wood, all the rides are hard surfaced and a series of paths offer ample opportunities to explore Castle Bytham's hidden corners. Remnants of the original ancient woodland can be found on the north east boundary which contains many statuesque boundary oaks.

The wood's northern edge is fascinating geologically with a number of shake and swallow holes in the limestone, while a nearby disused quarry supports a good variety of wildlife.

left:
Stapleford Wood

Stapleford Wood

NEWARK
A17 Coddington roundabout,
signposted Stapleford. (SK874551)
436HA (1,078 ACRES)
FORESTRY COMMISSION

Flat surfaces and a network of light, well-surfaced rides make Stapleford Wood a good choice for easy year-round walking.

This plantation is dominated by Scots and Corsican pine, with some pockets of spruce – although a walk to the western boundary reveals a woodbank and some veteran oaks. You can also enjoy pleasant views across pasture fields from the woodland edge.

The predominance of conifers means ground flora is relatively poor but the verges of the rides support a much wider variety of plants such as white clover, selfheal, sowthistle and creeping buttercup.

Stapleford Moor, a separate area of woodland just to the north is a quieter and less mature version of Stapleford Wood, having been established from scratch just after World War II.

High Wood

ANCASTER
From Sleaford take A17 towards Newark. After 3km (2 miles) turn left towards North Rauceby. At church turn right into Church Lane. High Wood is on right. Park in small car park in southern corner of wood. (TF010462)
13HA (32 ACRES)

Set atop a gently sloping hill overlooking the old Roman town of Ancaster and providing fine views, the aptly named High Wood is an important landscape feature in an otherwise poorly wooded area.

In spring the heart of the wood is ablaze with violets, thriving beneath young oak, ash, cherry and willow trees. There are relatively few mature trees in the centre of the wood but the outer edges are fringed with mature oak, ash and sycamore.

A surprising variety of butterflies have been recorded including purple hairstreak, white admiral and white-letter hairstreak – a species usually associated with elm.

Public access is good thanks to a network of paths. But go prepared with suitable footwear when it's wet – some paths can become quite muddy.

Southrey Wood

Bardney or Lincoln
Turn right off B1190 coming from Bardney to Bucknall. (TF129675)
103HA (255 ACRES)
Forestry Commission

Londonthorpe Wood and Alma Park

Grantham
From Grantham, follow signs towards Belton on A607. At Belton Garden centre turn right into Belton Village. Take first right and next right. Follow road and just before junction turn right into car park. (SK945379)
75HA (184 ACRES)
The Woodland Trust

below:
High Wood

above:
Tattershall Carrs

Tattershall Carrs

TATTERSHALL
From A153 Sleaford to Horncastle
Road turn north onto B1192 at
Conningsby. Wood is on left after 800m
(½ mile). (TF215590)
29HA (71 ACRES) SSSI
THE WOODLAND TRUST

Tattershall Carrs forms the
last remaining remnants of
ancient, wet, alder-dominated
woodland that once ringed
the margins of the Fens.

It also boasts a fascinating
history, for the wood was
used as an RAF base during
the Second World War – and
was home to the famous 617

'Dambusters' squadron. It's
still possible to make out
bomb shelters and structures
within the wood.

Designated a Site of Special
Scientific Interest (SSSI) as the
most extensive example of
ancient alder woodland on the
Lincolnshire fens, the site is in
fact two woods – Tattershall
Thorpe Carr and the larger
Tattershall Carr. Alder is particularly dominant in the
wetter, southern wood, the
two being linked by a narrow
green lane.

The woods make an attrac-
tive destination all year round
and contain a wealth of flora
and fauna including some
nationally scarce insect
species and a wide variety of

wild flowers. The regionally rare alternate-leaved golden saxifrage is present in the southern wood.

These are wet woods and the paths tend to be muddy in all but the driest of conditions.

The Pinewoods

WOODHALL SPA

Take B1191 towards Horncastle. Woodhall Spa lies along this road and The Pinewoods is on the left behind a row of shops. (TF194633)

8HA (19 ACRES)

THE WOODLAND TRUST

Once part of the landscaped grounds of the spa, the woodland is made up of mature oak, Scots pine, beech and a lot of regenerating birch. Decorative trees such as redwoods and limes have been introduced in the past.

The Pinewoods are favoured by lots of wildlife including a notable range of woodland birds. Great spotted woodpeckers nest in mature trees. The importance of protecting the site has been brought into focus when much of the woodland around the spa – which stands in a heavily farmed county – was lost to development.

It's a great place to enjoy a walk anytime of the year, but is particularly pleasant during spring and autumn. There is a well-used path network, generally very dry under foot.

Ostlers Plantation

WOODHALL SPA

Take B1191 north east in Woodhall Spa, then minor road east towards Kirkby on Bain. Car park is approx 800m (½ mile) outside Woodhall Spa on right. (TF215630)

136HA (336 ACRES)

FORESTRY COMMISSION

Ostlers Plantation is a post-war conifer plantation created on the site of the famous 'Dambuster' squadron airfield. Today, however, the site is one of tranquillity and beauty.

It's easy to explore, with no steep climbs and there are opportunities for youngsters to play among some interesting old pines. It's a good place to take a picnic, with benches scattered about the plantation.

The wood is almost entirely Corsican and Scots pine. On the ground you'll discover an abundance of bramble producing their ubiquitous and delicious crops of soft fruit in season.

above:
College Wood

College Wood

Lincoln
At Wragby take B1202 south, at
Kingthorpe turn right onto minor road.
Wood is approx 1.6km (1 mile) on right.
(TF120754)
64HA (158 ACRES)
FORESTRY COMMISSION

Dark and mysterious looking,
College Wood is part of the
Bardney Limewoods complex
and a wonderful place for children, with a special fairytale
quality.

The beauty of the woodland
soon emerges as you roam the
mix of pines, conifers, spruce,
oak, lime, ash and silver birch
that makes up a substantial
part of the original woodland.
One huge veteran oak in
particular provides an interesting highlight.

There are also alleys of limes
and ash on the site and there
are some young trees dotted
about the ancient woodland
section.

Resident wildlife includes
deer, squirrels, pheasant and
other birds as well as non-game
birds and owls. Look out too
for the deer tower. There is also
a good display of woodland
flora, particularly in the spring
and this is a wood that's particularly beautiful in winter.

Access through the site is
good, on well maintained rides
but wear sturdy shoes.

Chambers Farm Wood

Lincoln
Take B1202 south from Wragby to
Bardney – approx 5.6km (3½ miles).
Turn left along Hoop Lane and after
1.6km (1 mile) turn right to wood.
(TF149739)
34HA (83 ACRES) SSSI
FORESTRY COMMISSION

A walk through Chambers
Farm Wood provides a feast for
the senses and food for thought.

Set in the heart of the Bardney Limewoods, Chambers gained National Nature Reserve (NNR) status in 1997 – and this from a poorly wooded county. It is believed the site has been continuously wooded for thousands of years.

The main rides provide all-weather access for walkers and cyclists (in parts), serve plans for harvesting timber and enhance the unique limewood habitat.

Smaller paths provide ample opportunities to explore and the sharp-eyed can spot not only oak, ash and lime but also willow, alder, a rich shrub mix and even rarities such as the wild service tree.

The wide rides are managed to encourage butterflies, seen at their best in summer along a specially laid out 'butterfly walk'. Sensitively managed wetland areas support a variety of aquatic fauna and flora. Coppicing has reinvigorated the ground flora.

While the name of New Park Wood suggests the area has an ancient origin and may have been used for hunting deer and wild boar, little hard evidence remains on the site. Most of the woodland – mainly pine and spruce with oak and some small-leaved lime – was planted during World War II.

However, this is a pleasant wood with a well developed ride system. While there is no waymarking, the wood is quite open and navigation straightforward. Subsidiary routes can get extremely boggy following rain, so stout boots are recommended for your visit.

Why not combine your visit to New Park with a tour of its neighbours, which include Austacre Wood, currently being managed by the Forestry Commission under its Bardney Limewoods conservation plan.

New Park Wood

LINCOLN

Take A158 from Lincoln to Wragby, then B1202 to Bardney. Take minor road to Waddington. Wood is on sharp right after Lowfield Farm. (TF147705)

166HA (410 ACRES)

FORESTRY COMMISSION

left:
Newball Wood

Newball Wood

LINCOLN

A158 Langworth, going east, past public house and take right hand turn signposted falconry centre. Entrance to wood is approx 1.6km (1 mile) on left. (TF082757)

103HA (255 ACRES)

FORESTRY COMMISSION

You feel as though you're discovering an unknown corner of Lincolnshire on a visit to tranquil Newball Wood which can take you 3 hours to walk around.

Part of the Bardney Limewood area, the removal of conifers and subsequent regeneration of younger broadleaved trees on this ancient woodland site gives a very open feel. The main species are oak, lime, ash and willow. The reviving ground flora holds the promise of beautiful spring displays.

Bird and bat boxes dot the site – an 'I spy' test for youngsters – and just off the main ride by the entrance is an historical bonus, a moated structure similar to remains in nearby Cucklode Wood.

The main rides are good but can become boggy. You are unlikely to be disturbed by other visitors, but don't jump if you spot a large or exotic raptor – it's probably from the nearby falconry centre!

Hardy Gang Wood

LINCOLN

A158 going east, take right turn to falconry centre. Follow road for approx 3km (2 miles) and entrance is on right after sharp left turn. (TF090750)

35HA (87 ACRES)

FORESTRY COMMISSION

Hardy Gang Wood, a small and ancient wood, is currently enjoying a revival of fortunes. That's thanks to the Bardney Limewoods programme, designed to maintain and enhance the special qualities of the area which is now recognised as a unique and valuable relic of the past.

This site has a good variety with a pretty even spread of ash, oak, lime and birch. The wood is used for rearing pheasants and closes each Thursday during the shooting season.

Touring the site makes an interesting, 'hardy' walk along some clear and wide main rides though other routes are much narrower and can become difficult in the wet – so wellingtons are always a must.

Great West Wood

LINCOLN

Take A158 from Lincoln towards Wragby, then take a right towards Apley. Wood is on right before village. (TF105758)

86HA (213 ACRES)

FORESTRY COMMISSION

below:
Chambers Farm Wood (p.78)

Old Wood

LINCOLN
From Lincoln ringroad (A46 bypass)
travel west on B1378 to Skellingthorpe.
Wood is north west of Skellingthorpe.
(SK905725)
94HA (232 ACRES)
THE WOODLAND TRUST

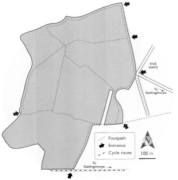

There's a real opportunity to enjoy the 'forest experience' on a visit to expansive Old Wood, an attractive and varied site with a mixture of ancient oak and lime woodland and conifers.

The ancient woodland has a high conservation value which will gradually develop further as the conifer areas, planted during the 1950s and 1960s, are replaced by native species.

The site boasts a wide variety of seasonal flora including twayblade, early-purple orchid, and the beautifully fragrant lily-of-the-valley. Historically the site was important for butterflies but the planting of conifers led to a decline in the butterfly population. However a wide variety of wildlife still exists within the wood, with owls and woodpeckers frequent visitors. Woodpeckers can often be heard at dusk and if you are lucky you may glimpse deer at quiet times.

Access to the wood is provided by a network of footpaths, cycleway, bridlepaths and public byways from the village of Skellingthorpe, 2.4km (1½ miles) away. Take care when navigating off the path network as it's quite easy to get lost.

Although there are some surfaced paths, other footpaths and bridleways have a tendency to become wet and muddy in the rain, so suitable footwear should be worn.

left:
Old Wood

above:
*Willingham
Woods (p.85)*

above:
Wickenby Wood

Wickenby Wood

<small>MARKET RASEN</small>
From A46 14.5 (9 miles) north east of
Lincoln, take minor road on sharp bend
to Friesthorpe. Go through village and
at T-junction turn right. Wood is on
right, before level crossing. (TF076824)
46HA (114 ACRES)
<small>FORESTRY COMMISSION</small>

Wickenby Wood is a welcoming yet tranquil wood, with a
wide stoned ride inviting you
through a variety of
broadleaved woodland including ancient woodland,
indicated by a bank and ditch.

Part of the Bardney
Limewoods complex, a group
of small-leaved lime lies
beyond the hazel-fringed ride.

Dead wood has been
retained to encourage mosses,
fungi and invertebrates and
you may spot bird and bat
boxes on your journey. It's
worth looking out for deer or
listening out for nightingale
song emerging from the dense
scrub. There is also a variety of
wetland habitats including
ponds and bog. The soil is clay
based and can be muddy –
don't forget your boots.

Shooting takes place on this
site. Check with the owner
before you visit.

Willingham Woods

MARKET RASEN

Take A631 east from Market Rasen. Car park is 800m (½ mile) past racecourse on left. (TF137884)

286HA (707 ACRES)

FOREST RY COMMISSION

Willingham Woods is the collective name for a group of post-war plantations that include Legsby, Osgodby, Usselby, Middle Rasen, Walesby and Dog Kennel Woods. These are working woods, mainly of Scots and Corsican pine, with regular felling – no two visits will ever be the same.

Well managed and equipped for high visitor numbers, the area is a popular spring and summer venue for weekend activities, most centred around the picnic area and car park.

Quieter times during the spring are good for discovering wildlife in the diverse range of grassland, wetland and woodland habitats. Well surfaced circular paths through the woodland provide the chance to go exploring and some of those paths are open to cyclists. The River Rase runs through the woods and in the centre of the site are the remains of a moat.

Eleanor Wood and Lynwode Wood

MARKET RASEN

Off the B1202 4km (2½ miles) south of Market Rasen. (TF120856)

41HA (101 ACRES)

FOREST RY COMMISSION

Eleanor Wood and Lynwode Wood are two very different neighbours linked together by a narrow strip, offering an interesting opportunity to compare and contrast. Formerly coniferous, Eleanor Wood is now open, with ash, oak, and some aspen. Great for picnics, it has a good ride and well-managed grass margins.

Contrast this with Lynwode, probably derived from Linden Wood, which still has a strong presence of lime trees throughout the site. Mature conifers are being removed and the areas recolonised by birch, hazel, lime and ash. In the spring you can find dense patches of bluebells in the north east corner.

You can still see the ancient woodbank from the edge of the east-west track, with great views across to the countryside beyond.

left:
Owlet Plantation

Owlet Plantation

GAINSBOROUGH
From A159 take turning towards
Laughton. In Laughton village turn left
and follow signs to Morton. Wood is on
left after approx 4km (2½ miles).
(SK825955)
50HA (125 ACRES)
THE WOODLAND TRUST

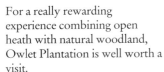

For a really rewarding
experience combining open
heath with natural woodland,
Owlet Plantation is well worth a
visit.

Birch, oak and pine areas are
interspersed among more open
heath while scattered throughout
the area you'll find mature oak
trees. Remnant heath vegetation
occurs on more open areas and is
home to a wealth of butterflies
like the brimstone, small copper
and purple hairstreak, giving
Owlet its Site of Nature
Conservation Interest status.

You might also catch a glimpse
of a nuthatch or a great spotted
woodpecker. All of this can be
enjoyed to the full by everyone,
thanks to a good circular and
surfaced all-abilities path.

There are a number of
informal paths across the site,
popular with local people and
those leading to the southern
section are particularly pleasant.
Not far away is a much larger
forested area known as
Laughton Forest and Laughton
Common, which links to Owlet
via a thin strip of woodland.

Laughton Forest

GAINSBOROUGH
Access via Tuetoes Hill between
Susworth and Laughton village.
(SE845017)
905HA (2,237 ACRES)
FORESTRY COMMISSION

Rigsby Wood

ALFORD
TURN NORTH TOWARDS SOUTH
THORESBY AT MILES CROSS HILL
CROSSROADS ON A1104 ROAD BETWEEN
ULCEBY CROSS AND ALFORD. WOOD IS
SET BACK ON RIGHT AFTER 2KM.
(TF421762)
15 HA (37 ACRES)
LINCOLNSHIRE WILDLIFE TRUST

Further Information

The Woodland Trust

Trees and forests are crucial to life on our planet. They generate oxygen, play host to a spectacular variety of wildlife and provide us with raw materials and shelter. They offer us tranquillity, inspire us and refresh our souls.

Founded in 1972, the Woodland Trust is now the UK's leading woodland conservation charity. By acquiring sites and campaigning for woodland it aims to conserve, restore and re-establish native woodland to its former glory. The Trust now owns and cares for over 1,000 woods throughout the UK.

The Woodland Trust wants to see:
* no further loss of ancient woodland
* the variety of woodland wildlife restored and improved
* an increase in new native woodland
* an increase in people's awareness and enjoyment of woodland

The Woodland Trust has over 100,000 members who share this vision. It only costs £2.50 a month to join but your support would be of great help in ensuring the survival of Britain's magnificent ancient woodland heritage. For every new member, the Trust can care for approximately another half acre. For details of how to join the Woodland Trust please ring FREEPHONE 0800 026 9650 or visit the website at www.woodland-trust.org.uk.

If you have enjoyed the woods in this book please consider leaving a legacy to the Woodland Trust. Legacies of all sizes play an invaluable role in helping the Trust to create new woodland and secure precious ancient woodland threatened by development and destruction. For further information please call 01476 581129.

Public Transport

Each entry gives a brief description of location, nearest town and a grid reference. Traveline provides impartial journey planning information about all public transport services by ringing 0870 608 2608 (minicom 0870 241 2216) (calls charged at national rates). For information about the Sustrans National Cycle Network ring 0117 929 0888.

Useful Contacts

The Forestry Commission, 0131 334 3047, www.forestry.gov.uk
The National Trust, 020 7222 9251, www.nationaltrust.org.uk
The Wildlife Trusts, 0870 036 7711, www.wildlifetrusts.org
RSPB, 01767 680551, www.rspb.org.uk
The Royal Forestry Society, 01442 822028, www.rfs.org.uk
The Woodland Trust, 01476 581111, www.woodland-trust.org.uk